STRATEGIES FOR JOINT VENTURES IN THE PEOPLE'S REPUBLIC OF CHINA

STRATEGIES FOR JOINT VENTURES IN THE PEOPLE'S REPUBLIC OF CHINA

Ike Mathur and Chen Jai-Sheng

PRAEGER

New York
Westport, Connecticut
London

Library of Congress Cataloging-in-Publication Data

Mathur, Iqbal.
    Strategies for joint ventures in the People's Republic
of China.

    Bibliography: p.
    Includes index.
    1. Joint ventures—China.   2. Investments, Foreign—
China.   3. China—Economic policy—1976–
4. China—Commercial policy.   I. Chen, Jai-Sheng.
II. Title.
HD62.47.M38   1987   3338.8'8851   87-7033
ISBN 0-275-92354-1 (alk. paper)

Library of Congress Catalog Card Number: 87-7033
ISBN: 0-275-92354-1

First published in 1987

Praeger Publishers, One Madison Avenue, New York, NY 10010
A division of Greenwood Press, Inc.

Printed in the United States of America

The paper used in this book complies with the
Permanent Paper Standard issued by the National
Information Standards Organization (Z39.48-1984).

10 9 8 7 6 5 4 3 2 1

Contents

Preface   vii

1 China and Joint Ventures   1

2 Chinese Socialist Ideology: Transformation and
   Construction   13

3 Chinese Socialist Ideology: Ownership and Wage
   Distribution   33

4 Chinese Economic Reforms   49

5 Market Planning in China   67

6 Pricing Mechanism in China   87

7 Chinese Foreign Trade   103

8 Regulatory Framework   121

9 Chinese Perspectives on Joint Ventures   133

10 The Chinese Joint Venture Law   143

11   Foreign Partner's Perspectives on Joint Ventures   161

12   Bargaining and Financing Considerations   177

Bibliography   187

Index   191

About the Authors   195

Preface

China's open door policy has not only allowed foreign firms to start joint ventures in China, but has also encouraged increased contact between academics in China and other countries. This higher level of contact has proved to be immensely beneficial for increased mutual understanding of vastly different economic systems. Thousands of scholars have crossed the Pacific in both directions to learn and to contribute their knowledge.

During the fall semester of 1985, the authors jointly conducted a doctoral seminar at Southern Illinois University on the theories of the multinational firm, the Chinese socialist economy, and joint ventures in China. The 12 participants—the 2 of us and 10 students—found the seminar to be an extremely valuable learning experience. This seminar provided the motivation for this book, which is partly based on our experiences with joint ventures in China.

Since 1978 many foreign firms have gone to China to establish joint ventures. Some of the ventures have been successful, while others have not turned out as planned. As we studied the successful and the less than successful joint ventures in China, we noticed

some similar patterns running throughout. Our emphasis in this
book is to provide information that can be effectively utilized to
negotiate joint ventures that are mutually beneficial for all partners
involved.

We express our gratitude to our families for providing us the
time to complete this work. We are grateful that Thomas G. Gut-
teridge, dean of the College of Business and Administration at
Southern Illinois University, arranged for the funding that made
our seminar feasible and provided moral support for completion
of this work. We thank Alison Podel at Praeger for her patience
with us during the initial writing stage. Finally, Laura Sims de-
serves a very special thank you for her attention to detail in typing
the manuscript.

accomplished, the Central Committee of the Chinese Communist Party established a general plan for the period of transition to socialism. It provided for the gradual realization of two tasks over a fairly long period of time, namely, the socialist industrialization of agriculture and handicrafts and the socialist transformation of capitalist industry and commerce. This general plan was announced in 1953 and was adopted and incorporated into the Constitution of the People's Republic of China at the First Session of the First National People's Congress in 1954.

The Socialist Transformation of Agriculture

After the land reform, the individual economy of the peasants became predominant in the countryside. Land reform emancipated the peasants from feudal exploitation and oppression and improved their lot. Their enthusiasm accounted for rises in farm production above preliberation levels. But the individual economy had its serious limitations. The 500 million peasants, more than 80 percent of the national population, were scattered in more than 110 million households. The households of former poor peasants and farmhands each had an average of about three-quarters of a hectare (11.7 mu or 1.93 acres) of land. There was only one draft animal in every 2 households, one plough in every 3 households, and one waterwheel in every 17 households. The middle peasants had an average of about 1.3 hectares (19 mu or 3.2 acres) of land, one plough, and less than one draft animal per household, and one waterwheel for every 7.5 households. The dispersed state of the peasants' economy precluded a rational use of land and the adoption of new farm tools. Productivity remained quite low.

Although the lot of peasants improved after the land reform, they were generally still not well-off, primarily because of the large population and the insufficient amount of farmland. The per capita cultivated area was one-fifth of a hectare (3 mu or .49 acres) across the country and one-fifteenth of a hectare (1 mu or .16 acres), or even less, in the southern provinces. Flood, drought, frost, windstorm, insects, and pests affected one part of the country or another every year, and the peasants had no way to combat these natural calamities.

A polarization between the rich and poor took place in the

countryside after land reform. Two factors were responsible: (1) the reform had not eliminated the economy of the rich peasants or the economic differences among the peasants, and (2) as small commodity producers, the peasants always had to depend on the market. Land was being sold by some peasants to others. Tenant farming and exploitation of hired labor reappeared. Usury and market speculation became serious problems throughout the country, and new rich peasants began to emerge. The individual peasants in China, particularly the poor peasants who formed the overwhelming majority of the rural population, looked to the Communist Party and the People's Government for leadership in starting agricultural cooperatives that would enable them to combat bad weather and increase farm productivity by building water conservancy projects and using farm machinery and other modern facilities. The poor peasants received land during the land reform, but they had few other means of production at their disposal. The collectives would have improved their conditions of production and emancipated them from the need to borrow money at high interest rates or to mortgage or sell their newly acquired land.

A sharp contradiction existed between the economy of small peasants and the program of industrialization. Agriculture constituted a large portion of China's economy. In 1952 agriculture accounted for 56.9 percent of the country's gross industrial and agricultural output value. Industry had to draw much of its raw material from agriculture and depended heavily on the rural market, and it was also necessary to accumulate part of the funds for industrialization by expanding farm production. The rising population in cities and industrial centers demanded an increasing amount of grain, vegetables, and other farm produce. Because of its low productivity and dispersed condition, the individual peasant economy could not meet the needs of industrialization. A shortage of farm produce became obvious as soon as full-scale industrial construction started in 1953. In the winter of the same year, the state implemented a plan whereby it became solely responsible for the buying and marketing of grain, cotton, and other major farm produce. This eased the contradiction between the individual peasant economy and industrialization but could not resolve it in a fundamental sense. Meanwhile, capitalism was competing with socialism for economic control over the countryside.

Thus, the socialist transformation of agriculture could not be delayed.

The campaign for mutual aid and cooperation had a long history. During the war years, the Communist Party led peasants in the revolutionary base areas in organizing mutual aid teams, which multiplied in the countryside after liberation. A small number of agricultural cooperatives were also organized as experiments before the movement for agricultural cooperation started in 1953.

The peasants, as small holders, had to be prepared gradually for a transition to public ownership. Three principles were adopted for the socialist transformation of agriculture: voluntariness and mutual benefit; persuasion by typical examples; and state assistance.

Organizationally, three steps were taken for the changeover. The first one was the mutual aid team. The participants in each team, ranging from several to a dozen households, retained their private ownership of land and other means of production. However, they worked together through an exchange of labor power, draft animals, and farm tools. The mutual aid team contained only an embryo of socialism.

The second step was the elementary agricultural producers' cooperative. Private ownership was kept intact, but lands were put together as investments, and income was distributed in proportion to the land invested and to the labor contributed in terms of both quality and quantity. The members were also reimbursed for the livestock, farm implements, and other means of production that they had invested. This was the semisocialist form of agricultural cooperation.

The third step was the advanced agricultural producers' cooperative. The cooperative had become fully socialist because land and other major means of production were now collectively owned, and income was distributed according to the labor contributed and nothing else.

The gradual advance from one form to another enabled the peasants to get used to collective production and changeover from private ownership to public ownership, avoiding or minimizing the losses that would have been caused by an abrupt change. Agricultural production rose year after year in the process. Taking the gross value of the agricultural production in 1952 as 100, it rose to 103.1 in 1953, to 106.6 in 1954, to 114.7 in 1955, and to 120.5 in 1957.

The economic status of the various strata of people in the countryside as well as their attitudes toward the socialist transformation were taken into consideration in the course of the agricultural cooperation movement. Initially, only the poor peasants and the lower stratum of the middle peasants (including poor peasants at the time of land reform who had become part of the lower stratum of middle peasants as well as those who had always belonged to the same stratum) were persuaded to join and were relied upon to run them well. The cooperatives eventually admitted the other middle peasants on a voluntary basis when they saw that participation would be beneficial for them. The policy toward the rich peasants' economy was one of gradual elimination through restriction. The rich peasants were not allowed to join until the cooperatives became firmly established. Admission was granted periodically to a group of rich peasants and landlords who had given up exploitation so that they might remold themselves into working people living by their own labor. This practice minimized obstruction and sabotage of the movement by landlords and rich peasants.

China's agricultural cooperation movement started in 1953. In the previous year only one in every thousand peasant households had joined the cooperatives even though there were a great number of mutual aid teams in the countryside. During the First Five-Year Plan period (1953–57) there was tremendous growth of mutual aid teams in the countryside, as well as in agricultural producers' cooperatives. Two percent of the households were in cooperatives in 1954. In July 1955 Chairman Mao delivered a report entitled "On the Cooperative Movement in Agriculture," resulting in an upsurge of the movement. Thereafter, agricultural cooperation developed very rapidly. By the end of the year, 14.2 percent of the peasants' households had joined the cooperatives, most of which were elementary ones with members drawing dividends on their land shares. By the end of 1956, 96.3 percent of the peasant households had joined the cooperatives, with 87.8 percent of them in advanced ones where land shares had been abolished and the members drew their pay on the exclusive basis of their labor contributions. Thus, by 1957 the socialist transformation of agriculture was basically completed.

In 1958 people's communes were set up throughout China. More than 740,000 agricultural producers' cooperatives were reorganized into more than 23,000 communes. The communes have gone through much readjustment and consolidation, and there are more than 54,000 of them in the countryside. But this transformation of agriculture has not suited the reality of China's economic situation. Practice showed that objective economic laws could not be violated. Too much was expected through a change in the relations of production, including ownership.

For a long time China was not sufficiently aware of the difficulties involved in the socialist transformation of an agricultural economy based chiefly on manual labor and the protracted nature of the task. Planners were often too anxious to cross from one stage to another and so caused losses to agricultural production. Socialism has to be based on large-scale socialized production. While China's realization of agricultural cooperation before mechanization was a rare achievement, it should have fully recognized that this was an immature, imperfect kind of socialism, which could not but retain vestiges of the old society. It should have made careful use of such imperfect socialism to develop agricultural productive forces and lay a solid material basis for a gradual improvement of the system. However, it did not see that the low level of productive forces was the main obstacle to the consolidation of collective ownership in agriculture.

The Socialist Transformation of Capitalist Industry and Commerce

In the early days of the People's Republic of China, the capitalist economy remained an important part of China's overall economy. There were 123,000 capitalist industrial enterprises employing 1.64 million workers, or 53.6 percent of the total number of industrial workers. Their gross output value came to 6.8 billion yuan ($1.5 billion), accounting for 48.7 percent of the country's gross output. The proportion taken up by private industry in the output of some major industrial products was as follows: 46.7

percent of cotton yarn, 40.3 percent of cotton cloth, 79.4 percent of flour, 80.4 percent of cigarettes, and 28.3 percent of the coal. A 1950 survey showed that there were 4.02 million private commercial enterprises (including small businesses) involving a total of 6.62 million persons. Their sales amounted to 18.2 billion yuan, accounting for 76 percent of national wholesale volume and 85 percent of the retail volume.

The capitalist economy played a dual role at the time. Because of China's lack of economic progress, the predominance of small-scale production, the difficulties involved in rehabilitating a war-ravaged economy, and the inability of the socialist state economy to meet all the needs in national construction and the people's living, capitalist industry and commerce remained a force that could play a supplementary role to the socialist state economy. By obtaining products from the capitalist industry, the state could exchange them for more grain, industrial raw materials, and farm produce from the peasants and keep adequate inventories for the market. This would help to strengthen the economic alliance between workers and peasants and stabilize prices. The capitalist enterprises, which employed a large number of technicians and managers, could be used to train more of them for national construction. A growth of the capitalist economy would also provide more funds for the state, which could take over part of the capitalist profit through taxation and pricing. The capitalist economy had an extensive network for domestic and foreign trade that could be used to stimulate the urban and rural economies and expand foreign trade. Such was the positive role that the capitalist economy could play in the national economy and people's life.

The capitalist economy also played a negative role because it was based on exploitation and completely profit oriented, serving as a means for the conversion of much social wealth into the private property of the capitalists. This dampened the enthusiasm for, and was thus harmful to, national construction and people's life. Competition and anarchy in production, the characteristics of capitalism, were bound to conflict with state plans. The profit motive of the capitalists, which often prompted their illegal actions, was destructive to economic development.

Unlike the bureaucrat-capitalist class or the feudal landlord class, however, the national bourgeois had a dual political character. In the period of the democratic revolution, it had a revolutionary side and a compromising side: it joined the revolution in certain circumstances and compromised with the enemy in others. In the period of the socialist revolution, it exploited the workers for profit, but it supported the Constitution of the People's Republic and was also willing to accept the socialist transformation.

In view of the dual role of the national capitalist economy and the dual character of the national bourgeois, the Chinese Communist Party and the People's Government adopted a policy of utilizing, restricting, and transforming capitalist industry and commerce.

For a certain period of time after the victory of the democratic revolution, the capitalist economy was allowed to exist and develop and was even given some benefits in matters like the supply of raw materials and the marketing of goods. Between 1949 and 1952, the gross output value of capitalist industry grew by 54 percent, and the retail sales volume in private commerce grew by 18.6 percent.

The state kept capitalist exploitation within certain limits by its taxation and pricing policies, labor insurance, and supervision over the distribution of the profits of capitalist enterprises. The government used both economic and administrative means to alleviate the anarchy in capitalist production and banned capitalist manipulation of the market, profiteering, and other unlawful activities. Due to the government reconstruction, a sharp struggle took place. In 1949 and 1952, taking advantage of the new republic's financial and economic difficulties, the capitalists generated four waves of rises on the resources of the state economy, defeated them on the market, and finally stabilized prices in the spring of 1950. In 1952 a campaign was launched against five crimes of law-breaking capitalists: bribery of government officials, tax evasion, cheating on government contracts, theft of state property, and stealing of economic information from government sources.

Two steps were taken to achieve socialist transformation. The first was a change from capitalism to state capitalism, and the second was a change from state capitalism to socialism. To give the capitalists sufficient time to adapt themselves to socialist transformation, a gradual transition was effected in the change from capitalism to state capitalism. At a lower level of state capitalism, capitalist enterprises in industry processed materials supplied by the government for marketing, and those in commerce acted as sales agents for state commerce. At the higher level of state capitalism, the capitalist enterprises were placed under joint state-private ownership.

In industry, since the government controlled large quantities of raw materials, it started in 1950 to direct private enterprises into the orbit of state capitalism by providing them with material for processing, placing orders with them, or buying up and marketing all their products. In 1954 it began to place capitalist factories and mills under joint state-private ownership.

In commerce, since the government controlled the main sources of commodities through the state and cooperative commerce, it was able to conduct wholesale business with private stores on its terms and let them handle retail business on commission. By 1954 this rudimentary form of state capitalism was well established, and the socialist transformation of the capitalist industry and commerce accelerated. The upsurge in the cooperative movement in agriculture in the second half of 1955 made capitalist development almost impossible in the countryside and tipped the balance in favor of the working class in its struggle with the capitalists. This led to an upsurge in the socialist transformation of capitalist industry and commerce. Joint state-private ownership, which had existed only in individual enterprises, now embraced whole trades. By the end of 1956, the system covered 99 percent of the capitalist industrial enterprises and their workers and 99.8 percent of their output value. Eighty-two percent of the private commercial enterprises had become state-private ones. Under state capitalism, the means of production formerly owned by the capitalists were used or distributed by the state in a unified way. Except for the fact that the capitalists still drew fixed interest incomes on their socialized assets, the joint enterprises showed practically no differences from state enterprises. Thus, the socialist transformation of capitalist industry and commerce was basically completed.

To reach the goal of socialism through a peaceful transformation of capitalism, China adopted a policy of gradual redemption in socializing the means of production owned by the capitalists. At the stage of state capitalism, redemption was effected through the distribution of profits. In other words, the capitalists were given a certain percentage of the profits of the enterprises. At the time, the profits of an enterprise were divided into the following four parts: income tax; the public accumulation fund of the enterprises; a public welfare fund for equipment replacement; and profit for the capitalists, including the interest on the shares and the dividends. The profit left for the capitalists usually accounted for 25 percent of total profits. After the enterprises were placed under joint state-private ownership by whole trades, redemption took the form of fixed interest. In other words, over a certain period of time, the state paid private shareholders fixed interest, usually at an annual rate of 5 percent, regardless of the actual income of the enterprises. The private shares in enterprises under state-private ownership were valued at 2.4 billion yuan, and the state paid 1.14 million private shareholders about 120 yuan as fixed interest every year. The government first announced that the fixed interest would be paid over a period of seven years, that is, from January 1, 1956, to the end of 1962. In 1962 the period was extended for three more years from the beginning of 1963. Payment actually stopped in 1967.

After the changeover to state-private ownership, all those previously on the management of capitalist enterprises were assigned suitable work by the government, and those who could not work were properly taken care of, some through relief. This was also part of the policy of redemption. A survey in 1957 showed that the 710,000 private shareholders drawing fixed interest and the 100,000 former members of the capitalist managerial staff were all given jobs. Among them 60 to 65 percent were directly engaged in production of business operation, while 35 to 40 percent were given managerial jobs. They also retained their high wages.

The socialist transformation of the capitalist economy was combined with the remolding of the capitalists. Through political education, the government helped the capitalists to change themselves from exploiters to working people earning their living by their own labor.

Socialist Transformation and Socialism

The socialist transformation of agriculture, industry, and commerce brought a fundamental change to China's socioeconomic

structure. By the end of 1956, the socialist economic system had
been established. The features of this system are as follows: (1)
public ownership of the means of production, including socialist
ownership by all the people in the state economy, and socialist-
collective ownership by the working people in the collective economy; (2) the implementation of the principle of "from each according to his work" on the basis of the public ownership of the
means of production and, consequently, the elimination of exploitation; and (3) a planned economy based on the public ownership of the means of production.

The Chinese Communist Party found a creative way to carry
out the socialist transformation given China's conditions. Thus,
China accomplished a fundamental change in the socioeconomic
system without social and economic turmoil and destruction of
the productive forces, which are usually unavoidable in similar
circumstances. On the contrary, socialist transformation helped the
growth of productive forces and of the economy. Between 1953
and 1956, the country registered an average annual increase of 19.6
percent in gross industrial output value and 4.8 percent in gross
agricultural output value.

However, the socialist transformation in China also had its
shortcomings and deviations. Beginning in the summer of 1955,
there was much rashness in pushing the cooperative movement in
agriculture and the changeover in the individual sectors of handicrafts and commerce. The speed was too fast and the form too
unitary, leaving behind some problems that remained unsolved
for a long time. After the basic completion of the socialist transformation of the capitalist industry and commerce, some of the
former industrialists and businessmen were not properly used or
taken care of. However, it should be recognized that the task of
socialist transformation was not easy, given a population of 700
million people.

SOCIALIST CONSTRUCTION

China's efforts at industrialization and economic development
are discussed in this section.

Socialist Industrialization and Economic Development

While the strategies for socialist economic development are significant theoretical and policy issues in socialist modernization that require resolution, they have not been properly addressed for a long time. Particularly, China is a country with an enormous population and vast territory whose economy has been undeveloped, so it needs to explore through practice and find out how to carry out socialist modernization.

At the time of China's First Five-Year Plan, although certain shortcomings in blindly copying Soviet methods did exist, the course of socialist industrialization was, generally speaking, relatively healthy. When the First Five-Year Plan was drafted, the requirements of the basic economic laws of socialism and of the laws of the planned proportional development of the national economy were studied under the guidance of Marxist theory, and at the same time China's actual conditions were given serious consideration. As socialist industrialization is the major part of China's socialist construction, the First Five-Year Plan gave primary emphasis to heavy industry, based on China's conditions at that time. In addition, it clearly stipulated that efforts were to be made to preserve the appropriate proportion between the various economic sectors, especially industry and agriculture, and heavy and light industry. In view of the need for substantial funding for large-scale construction as well as the necessity for the goal of socialist production to satisfy the needs of the people, the First Five-Year Plan also stipulated that consideration should be given to both accumulating funds and improving the livelihood of its citizens. In other words, attention had to be paid to expanding the accumulation of funds, while at the same time the people's material and cultural levels were to be raised gradually. Due to the rational and effective implementation of the First Five-Year Plan, the economy then developed rapidly, and workers and peasants also benefited materially.

In summing up the practical experience of its First Five-Year Plan, China realized that the Soviet model emphasized heavy industry and neglected agriculture and light industry. As a result, goods in the market were inadequate. The policies that the Soviet model emphasized, such as compulsory sales to the state, took away too much from the peasants, and the prices they got were too low. Accumulation of funds in this way did great damage to the peasant's initiative in production.

However, starting in 1958 under the influence of a "leftist" guiding ideology, the strategy for China's economic development changed for the worse. The positive experiences of the First Five-Year Plan period were not consistently upheld, and the resolutions of the Eighth Party Congress as well as other sound policies were not carried out. On the contrary, strategic goals and measures not in accordance with China's actual situation were proclaimed. In the Great Leap Forward, the strategy of "overtaking and surpassing" was unrealistic; it sought a pace of economic development unsuited to the situation. As a result, the national economy suffered serious dislocation, industrial and agricultural production declined, economic efficiency significantly worsened and the people's livelihood experienced severe difficulties. In the winter of 1960 the Party's Central Committee decided to adjust the national economy by adopting the principles of "readjustment, consolidation, filling out and raising standards." The task of readjustment was basically completed by 1965. However, the "leftist" guiding ideology still had not been thoroughly corrected but continued to develop during the ten years of the Cultural Revolution. Errors in this area, compounded by other misjudgments, had caused damage to China's national economy once again, only this time even worse than before. More recent economic reforms are discussed in Chapter 4.

Present Stage of Socialism

The guiding ideology of China's socialist construction is derived from scientific theories on the basic system of socialist economic forms, such as public ownership of the means of production and distribution according to work. But no one could give an exhaustively detailed blueprint for socialism. This question could only be answered through practice. Furthermore, due to differences in various countries' concrete conditions and levels of economic development, actual methods of socialist construction would necessarily vary, and thus different models of socialism would appear. For a long time, the dominant theory in socialist countries was that the property structure and economic management system that took shape in the Soviet Union in the late 1920s and early 1930s was the only acceptable model under socialist conditions. China was no exception. Production and exchange methods were gradually established using the Soviet models. However, due to the influence of a "leftist" guiding ideology, in addition to the use of the Soviet models, China committed quite a lot of serious errors with negative aftereffects on the development of the national economy.

After the Third Plenum of the Eleventh Party Congress, the Chinese Communist Party adopted principles for the reform of China's property structure and economic management system, in accordance with the Marxist tenet that the production functions should suit the conditions of the forces of production. The principles that were adopted all originated in practice, were fully responsive to the masses' creativity, and were explored through investigative studies and by summing up the experiences of the masses. The Party's Central Committee explicitly proclaimed that a fixed mode for the development of socialist production functions did not exist, and the task was to create concrete forms for the production functions that met the needs of the productive forces at each stage. Furthermore, such forms would have to be developed on a continual basis. While ownership by the whole people and collective ownership are the basic economic forms, at the same time China should permit, within limits, the existence and development of an individual economy of working people as a necessary supplement to the public economy in order to suit the conditions of China's productive forces and benefit the development of production. China should also adopt concrete management and distribution systems appropriate to the actual conditions of the various economic sectors.

A planned economy should be carried out on the basis of socialist public ownership within the scope of the whole national economy, and a proportional coordinated development of the national economy should be guaranteed through the overall balance of the planned economy and the supplementary role of market regulation. Since 1981 China's economic reforms, especially in agriculture, have already made great progress due to the government's adherence to this Marxist principle.

The Third Plenum of the Eleventh Party Congress first grasped this key link in agriculture. It emphasized overcoming the longstanding "leftist" errors in the guiding ideology of the past, respecting the autonomy of the production unit, restoring private plots, household sideline production and rural fairs, and gradually introducing many forms of the production responsibility system. At the same time, the Third Plenum raised the procurement price of grain and other agricultural products and then resolved the principles for diversified economy, thereby rapidly and visibly changing the face of China's agriculture. Thus, agriculture's original stagnation was transformed into flourishing prosperity, promoting a turn for the better in the entire economic and even political situation.

The contract system of responsibility linked to production holds the crucial position in the series of extremely effective measures adopted by the Communist Party in agriculture. This system employs the principle of combining unified and decentralization operations, bringing into play simultaneously the individual initiative of the contracting parties and the superiority of the collective system. Fully affirming and truly respecting the position of China's hundreds of millions of peasants as both workers and managers in this way greatly increases both their initiative in the management of production and their sense of responsibility as being masters of their own work. It also cures the long-standing malady of eating from "one big pot" and making "a great hullabaloo" and guarantees that Chinese productive capacity will develop swiftly. Promoting the perfection and the development of the contract responsibility system will help China to find the form of collective ownership suited to the level of development of productive forces and make the actual path of the socialist collectivization of agriculture more appropriate to China's realities.

China's rural economy at present is developing toward socialization on the basis of contract responsibility. Following further practice of the contract responsibility system, specialized and key households are springing up in great numbers, and commercial production in the countryside is constantly increasing. All these have brought forth an urgent need for various services, such as product merchandising and processing, storage and transport, and dissemination of new techniques and information. This kind of economic activity, gradually separating from family (or small group) contracts, will operate in the form of unified management and expanded cooperation and meanwhile will enrich its content. Having drawn a lesson from the past, this kind of economic cooperation, based on the contractual specialization and division of work and occupation, is not predicated on a return to the original restrictive combinations of production teams, brigades, and communes. Rather, a combination that promotes specialization and socialization by focusing on the need to develop the production and exchange of commodities is required. The forms of combination will be many and varied. For example, they may be small-scale combinations that develop among the peasantry or specialized households, or ones that result from the framework set up top-down by state structures in commerce, supply and distribution, agricultural and animal husbandry departments, and so on, and develop in the process of serving and establishing links with the peasantry. The peasant family (or small group) contractual economy will be integrated with the state-run economy through these various forms, and their primary economic activities will be channeled into the state plan through such means as the contract system. Implementing the contract responsibility system linked to production not only opened up a correct path for the socialist development of agriculture but also contributed extremely practical and enlightening experiences for instituting a variety of forms of the responsibility system in the management of state-run industrial and commercial enterprises.

CONCLUSIONS

There are many practical lessons from China's experiences in carrying out socialist economic construction. The ones discussed are of particular interest.

Production must take the satisfaction of the people's needs as its goal. Socialist production must strive to satisfy directly the ever-increasing material and cultural needs of the people. The tendency to produce for the sake of production, which existed for a long time in the past, damaged economic construction and the livelihood of the citizenry. In the future, production and the people's livelihood have to be planned as a whole, proceeding from the idea of "everything for the people."

The relationship between output and proportion must be properly handled. The Marxist theory of production indicates that to carry out social production smoothly, coordinated and rational proportionate relations between the two major sectors and within each sector as well as between accumulation and consumption must be established. However, for a long time, China one-sidedly emphasized output and neglected proportion and considered that the proportion should be subordinate to output. Proportionality is a precondition for rapid development of the national economy. In the process of implementing industrialization, it is necessary to give priority to the development of heavy industry under certain conditions. However, attention should also be paid to the development of agriculture and light industry. They should be placed in important positions and heavy industry made to serve them.

The relationship between output and efficiency must be properly handled. In the past a high rate of output was one-sidedly sought and economic efficiency was neglected. Although the general output increased, the increase of accumulation and improvement of the people's livelihood was affected by discrepancies in economic efficiency. From now on the emphasis is on attainment of better economic results, and output must be established on the basis of these better economic results.

In summing up the experience of China's socialist construction, there is one other point that is extremely important. Generally speaking, it is easy to suggest plans for development that greatly exceed objective possibilities. So, this is the reason why China's economic development repeatedly experienced setbacks. China's basic national situation has determined that a strategic concept of protracted struggle is correct for economic construction, while that of "rapid successes" is completely wrong. Severe losses have been suffered more than once in the past from the strategy of rapid successes. This is a manifestation of the "leftist" guiding ideology whose influence must be resolutely wiped out from now on.

Since 1979 China's strategy for economic development has undergone a new turn; that is, the thorough purge of the "leftist" guiding ideology and the insistence on adopting a strategy for economic development that is feasible, scientifically based, and suited to China's national conditions. The government proclaimed the principle that the urgent tasks for the whole country would focus on improving economic efficiency and advance on a new path of economic construction.

A review of China's socialist economic construction clearly reveals that, if China can uphold the integration of the universal truth of Marxism with its own concrete realities and establish a path of its own, then it will certainly be able to transform itself into a strong, modernized socialist country with Chinese characteristics.

3

Chinese Socialist Ideology: Ownership and Wage Distribution

After the Chinese revolution in 1949, the government started the process of converting private enterprises to state-owned enterprises. In the industrial and commercial sectors of the economy, this process has largely been completed, resulting in the ownership of the means of production by people as a whole. Collective ownership, considered to be an inferior form of ownership in a socialist system, is predominant in the Chinese agricultural sector. The first part of this chapter explains in detail these two forms of ownership, as well as the two resultant classes of laborers—workers and peasants.

The second part of this chapter deals with the Chinese wage distribution system. The principle of "to each according to his work" is explained within the context of Chinese socialist ideology. Various aspects of the Chinese wage system are also discussed in this chapter.

SOCIALIST OWNERSHIP

In China ownership refers to owning the means of production. Starting in 1956, socialist ownership took two different forms:

ownership by the whole people and collective ownership in the cooperatives. Between the revolution and 1967, the Chinese government paid fixed payments to private industrialists and businessmen operating joint state-private enterprises. In 1967 these state-private enterprises were converted to state enterprises. Since 1979 the Chinese government has encouraged individual initiative, and a small but growing number of enterprises are now operated by individuals.

Ownership by the whole and collective ownership are both socialist forms of ownership. The difference between the two forms can be attributed to the degree of development of socialism. Ownership by the whole people represents a higher form of socialist public ownership. Under this form of ownership, the means of production belong to all the working people; that is, the means of production are essentially the public property of society as a whole. Production is carried out by the state plan and is aimed at fulfilling the rising material and cultural requirements of society.

Collective ownership is a lower form of social public ownership under which the means of production are not yet the public property of society as a whole but belong to the working people in one economic cooperative or another. In the economic sector under collective ownership, production is carried on with the leadership and support of the socialist state economy, and the main economic operations are geared to the needs of the government and the people through state planning and other economic measures. The exchange of products between the state and the cooperatives must basically conform to the principles of equal exchanges. Thus, the collective economy is a socialist economy in which there is no exploitation of one by another.

Accumulation and Consumption Funds

At the present time, both systems of ownership—by the whole people and collective—coexist and share somewhat similar procedures for distributing revenues in excess of expenses. The surplus is divided into two portions: an accumulation fund and a consumption fund. The accumulation fund is handled by the state according to unified state plans and policies. The consumption fund, as the nomenclature implies, is distributed to the workers. The consumption fund for state enterprises is distributed to the staff and workers of the enterprises. For cooperatives, after allocation to the state accumulation fund, the balance is divided between a consumption fund and an accumulation fund for the cooperative. Members of a cooperative share among themselves their consumption fund and do not receive anything from the consumption fund in the sector under ownership by the whole people.

Different cooperatives have different means of production. Differences in the quantity and quality of the means of production, as well as differences in natural and economic conditions, result in wide differences in labor productivity, output, and income. Since the cooperatives are responsible for their own profits and losses, the pay of cooperative workers varies from one cooperative to another. The pay scale system that is utilized by state enterprises is not copied by the cooperatives. Also, differences in the funds accumulated by cooperatives determine differences in their capacity for expanded and extended production.

Two Types of Working People

The two systems of ownership of the means of production account for the existence of two types of working people in China—workers and peasants. In China industry is dominated by ownership by the whole people, while agriculture is dominated by collective ownership. The workers are generally considered to represent workers in ownership by the whole people, while the peasants are often regarded as representative of workers in cooperatives.

The existence of the two systems of socialist public ownership in socialist society within a given period is determined by the level of development of productive forces. Industrial production in China is basically mechanized, and a number of industries are highly mechanized and are rapidly moving toward automation. However, agricultural production is still conducted mainly by manual labor and the use of draft animals, and mechanization has begun in only a few rural areas. Because of these different levels of productive forces, industrial production generally shows a relatively strong social character, as manifest in the complex division of labor and cooperation among the various departments and enterprises. This gives rise to an objective need for society and the state to own the industrial means of production directly and to exercise centralized, unified leadership over industrial production. In other words, it calls for a system of socialist ownership by the whole people. On the other hand, agricultural production shows a relatively weak social character, since a considerable portion of the production of a cooperative is consumed by itself and by its members. In such circumstances, collective ownership facilitates production and management and brings into play the socialist enthusiasm of the members of such a unit. It is a form of ownership that answers the need for developing productive forces in agriculture.

Due to differences in the levels of product inputs and labor productivity between industry and agriculture, disparities in the standard of living between the workers and the peasants cannot be eliminated within a short period. Differences in the conditions of material production and in labor productivity among collective economic units, coupled with the distribution of products within each collective, result in considerable disparities in wages and living standards among the peasants of different collectives. To affect distribution among the workers and peasants on the single basis of equal pay for equal work, the most appropriate thing to do is to bring up the incomes of the peasants gradually to the level of the workers' wages, rather than to resort to egalitarianism. The proper way to eliminate the differences in the incomes of peasants of different collectives is by raising the lower incomes and not by leveling off those that are higher. Peasants account for more than 80 percent of China's population. It is obviously impossible to raise the living standard of the peasants all at once—especially of those in low-yield communes and brigades—to the level of the workers without a protracted effort to achieve a tremendous growth in the industrial and agricultural production.

Issues Related to Form of Ownership

Ownership by the whole people and collective ownership create some contradictions. These include the contradictions between the working class and the peasants and between the state and the collectives, for instance, the contradiction over taxation, the quantities of agricultural produce purchased by the state, and the purchasing prices. If the agricultural tax levied by the state on the collectives is too heavy, it will reduce the funds accumulated by the collectives and will affect the income of the peasants. Excessive purchasing and underpricing are also harmful to the interests of the collectives and the incomes of the peasants. The state, in general, seeks to establish correct policies with regard to taxation, the purchase of agricultural produce, and the price of industrial and agricultural goods, taking into consideration the interests of both the state and the collectives. The idea behind the policies is to effect a rapid development of industrial and agricultural production and of the economy as a whole. Since the founding of the People's Republic of China, the agricultural tax has remained low, but there were years in which too much grain was purchased from peasants, causing dissatisfaction among them. Today the difference between industrial and agricultural prices is still much in favor of industry, and effective measures are being taken to change the situation. If correct policies are adopted, these contradictions can certainly be handled in a way that will benefit the consolidation and development of the socialist economic system.

Ownership by the Whole People at the Present Time

An enterprise under socialist ownership by the whole people is accountable to the state, which represents the interests of the whole people; it must protect state property, carry out the production plans formulated by the state, and conduct the distribution and exchange of products according to state assignments. At the same time, the management or managerial body is accountable to the workers of the enterprise and must take care of their interests and promote a steady improvement in their livelihood along with the growth in production. The socialist state carries out the principle of "to each according to his work" among the workers, who are concerned with their own personal interests as well as the interests of the state. These two kinds of interests should in principle be identical, because increases in production and state revenue will eventually result in higher incomes for the workers. However, such an identity of interests does not manifest itself in such a direct manner as in a collective enterprise, which is responsible for its own profits and losses. If the managers do not concern themselves with the livelihood of the workers and fail to improve it, the workers will not concern themselves with the enterprise and the state, but treat them with the mentality of wage laborers.

The managerial system of industry in China, borrowed from the Soviet Union in the 1950s, puts undue emphasis on centralized leadership by the state. The manager or managerial body of an enterprise is accountable for its performance only to the state but not to the workers of the enterprise. The manager is not elected by the workers but appointed by a higher state organ. The workers contribute labor and draw pay in accordance with the state plan without a full right to the management of the enterprise or any extra benefit from its production increase. Although the Communist Party has repeatedly called for broadening the workers' democratic rights and for their participation in management, little has been achieved because no specific measures have been taken or the measures adopted are mere formalities.

Such a system of economic management deprives the workers and the enterprises of their rights to handle their own affairs. All the economic operations of an enterprise are dictated by state plan. An enterprise has to depend on state allocations for investment, even for technical innovation funds, and must turn over all profits to the state. An enterprise has no direct contact with the market because all purchasing and marketing is generally conducted by state commercial departments, and the transfer of workers and staff members from one enterprise to another is up to the labor departments of the government. In other words, an enterprise has little control over human, material, and financial resources or over the procurement of material for production and marketing and is hardly able to play its proper role as a basic unit of economic management. This makes it difficult for an enterprise to take the initiative in improving technology and management, raising labor productivity, and thus increasing its contributions to the state and the people. Such a system hardly encourages workers, from the angle of their financial interests, to increase production by achieving the maximum economic results with the minimum expenditure of labor and material resources, or to raise their own standard of living by increasing the income of the enterprise.

Collective Ownership at the Present Time

Socialist collective ownership is a form of transition from individual ownership to ownership by the whole people. In China the transition was effected in two steps: a change from individual ownership to collective ownership and a change from collective ownership to ownership by the whole people. The two stages are interconnected but different in nature. The first step means a transition from private ownership to public ownership, involving an alteration in the relation of production, which must keep pace with the growth of productive forces. The second step involves moving from a lower form of socialist public ownership to a higher one, which requires, first of all, a tremendous growth of productive forces. China's peasants, who account for 80 percent of the population, still live under a system of collective ownership that is predominant in agriculture. The rural collectives, that is, the people's communes, generally follow a three-level system of ownership of the means of production: ownership by commune, by the production brigade, and by the production team, with the last as the basic form. A production team, as a basic accounting unit, is usually composed of an average of 30–40 households and carries on production mainly by manual labor and the use of draft animals. Thus, collective ownership in China today is a lower form of socialist public ownership.

It is necessary to have a collective ownership system in China because of the extremely low level of productive forces, the varying farming conditions, and the wide gaps in labor productivity between different areas, communes, and production brigades and teams. The state can neither raise the pay in low-yielding teams to that in high-yielding ones, nor can it reduce the latter. If the state were to take from those who have more and give to those who have less as a means to even up the incomes, the high-yielding teams would be unwilling to strive for still higher yields, while the low-yielding ones would not try to catch up. This would seriously hamper the growth of agricultural production.

An important reason for a far lower labor productivity in agriculture than in industry is that the former has to depend on natural conditions, and mechanization of agricultural production is more difficult than industrialization. The equipment for farm mechanization has to come from industry. Labor productivity in agriculture cannot rise significantly unless industry produces more, better, and cheaper farm machinery. Industrialization started in capitalist countries as early as the latter part of the eighteenth century, made rapid progress early in the twentieth century, and reached the level of modernization soon afterward. On the other hand, mechanization of agricultural production did not take place until the beginning of the twentieth century. Its standards were gradually improved after the 1940s and became relatively high only after the 1950s. With a huge population, a small per capita amount of farmland, a low pay for work, and highly priced farm machinery, China faces far greater difficulties in mechanizing its agriculture than the United States and West European countries did. Although initial progress has been achieved in farm mechanization in some areas in China, it has not led to a significant increase in agricultural labor productivity or in farm output. In particular, production costs of agricultural produce have gone up in many areas because of greater input prices, creating a situation in which a higher output is not accompanied by a higher income. Thus, it is necessary to improve management and achieve better economic results with farm mechanization, so as to ensure a quick rise in agricultural labor productivity and in output and income.

Agriculture lags far behind industry in the division of labor and coordination. In fact, China's agriculture remains in a state of partial self-sufficiency, with roughly three-fourths of the grain, the main produce, consumed by the peasants themselves. The peasants also produce some of their means of production, such as seed grains, fodder, and organic manure, and breed some of the draft animals. The greater the extent of self-sufficiency, the smaller the scope for the unified management of production and distribution. This is also one of the reasons why the size of a collective economic unit cannot be very large at the present stage. There will, however, be a gradual change in the situation when the collectives are brought closer together through farm mechanization and the growth of those industries that are operated by communes and production brigades and teams.

WAGE DISTRIBUTION SYSTEM UNDER SOCIALISM

Under the socialist system, the means of production are the public property of the whole society or that of a collective. The workers are the owners of the means of production and no longer separated from them. They jointly own, manage, and use the means of production and engage in production together. Society requires that all its able-bodied members contribute their work ability to it or to their collective and assigns them jobs commensurate with their ability.

The conversion of the means of production into public property under socialism cannot immediately eliminate the workers' possession of their labor power. The worker continues to regard labor as a means of earning a living and cannot possibly work for society without consideration of salary. If he or she is to work for society irrespective of compensation, society must provide the worker and dependents with all necessary means of subsistence free of charge. Obviously, this is something beyond the capability of a newborn socialist society in which the productive forces are not yet fully developed. Since society is still unable to provide its members with a free supply of all necessary means of subsistence, it can pay workers only on the basis of the quantity and quality of work they perform, leaving it to them to work out the family budget. Besides, the division between mental and physical labor continues to exist in a socialist society, while the needs of highly educated mental workers in their work and daily life call for special attention. All these factors indicate that worker power remains partly a personal possession of the worker.

In socialism the workers are joint owners of the means of production, and the relationship between the workers and society becomes one of the individual and the collective owning the same means of production; that is, there is no longer a relationship between two different owners of two different things. On the other hand, since society has to tacitly recognize unequal productive capacities as natural privileges of individuals, which presupposes the exchange of equal amount of work for an equal amount of products between society and the individual worker, the society and the individual worker remain, in this sense, different owners. In these circumstances, the means of production are united with labor power in a unique manner; while all the working people form a productive community by the use of jointly owned means of production, each person receives pay on the basis of the quantity and quality of his or her labor.

Public ownership of the means of production and partial possession of labor power by the individual constitute a contradiction that gives socialist labor a dual nature. On the one hand, because the worker is one of the joint owners of the means of production, his or her labor takes on a direct social character. On the other hand, labor power remains a personal means of livelihood. This dual nature of socialist labor is discernible everywhere in Chinese life.

The most striking expression of the dual nature of socialist labor, however, is the distribution of products. Under the socialist system, social products are already the public property of society or of the collectives and are distributed by society. Some of these are reserved for the common needs of society, while the rest are distributed among the individual workers on the basis of the quantity and quality of their labor for their daily needs and those of their families, giving rise to the individual ownership of the means of subsistence. Labor in the first category is performed by the worker for society, while labor in the second category is performed by the worker for himself or herself. The division between labor performed for society and that performed for the worker is an expression of the dual nature of socialist labor in the field of distribution.

To Each According to His Work

In China the system of "to each according to his work" was gradually established during the development of the socialist economy following the proletarian seizure of power. Several systems of ownership of means of production were in existence immediately after the founding of the People's Republic of China. The capitalist system of distribution had to continue in capitalist enterprises. In socialist enterprises, the labor contract system, the indentured labor system, and other forms of feudal exploitation were abolished while the old wage system was kept intact. As production developed, wages of manual laborers were steadily raised. The First Five-Year Plan initiated in 1953 included a new eight-grade wage system based on the principle of "to each according to his work" as well as a post/rank salary system for government and managerial personnel who are paid according to their ranks and posts. In the interest of greater unity with managerial personnel from preliberation days, the government did not subject them to the new pay scale, but paid them retained salaries that were relatively close to their preliberation income and higher than the regular salaries for their ranks and posts. Such salaries were not entirely based on the principle of "to each according to his work" but were partially paid as redemption to the bourgeoisie.

Practicing the system of "to each according to his work" in a socialist society means recognition of the material interests of the individual, a principle that provides for unequal pay for workers with unequal productive capacities and unequal labor contributions. At this stage, it is essential to provide the working people with material as well as moral incentives. The greater one's ability and contributions, the greater one's pay. In this way, the interests of the individual and those of the collectives and the state merge in a way to foster enthusiasm among the working people and stimulate the development of productive forces. The present differences in pay will not exist indefinitely. Recognition of differences is a means of achieving a high rate of growth for productive forces, thus allowing for an eventual elimination of wage differentials. At the present time, egalitarianism, in which salaries would be set regardless of quantity and quality of work, would dampen people's enthusiasm and hinder the development of productive forces, making it difficult to implement the gradual transition to the practice of "to each according to his needs."

Some Important Wage Policies in China

The wage system must follow the principle of "to each according to his work," that is, the principle of more pay for more work and less pay for less work, avoiding both wide discrepancies in wages and none at all. The wage system left over from prerevolutionary China showed wide disparities in the salaries of blue-collar workers. Such unjustifiable differences have gradually been lessened through reforms and readjustments of the wage system. For more than two decades, the Chinese principle has been one of "no raises for the upper income brackets, fewer raises for the medium income brackets and more raises for the lower income brackets." In the past decade, more egalitarianism has become the major tendency in handling of wages. Egalitarian ideas in China have a broad base and deep historical roots. As an economically underdeveloped country in the process of modernization, China was forced to adopt a low pay scale that, coupled with a failure to affect pay raises for years, made life difficult for many middle-aged workers and staff members. In these circumstances, whenever pay raises are considered or bonuses granted, priority is often given to the most hard-pressed ones, making it difficult to abide by the principle of "to each according to his work." Elimination of the egalitarianism prevalent among both cadres and the masses will be difficult, but it is being attempted patiently. Its continued influence prevents both the principle of to each according to his or her work and the modernization drive from being effectively carried out.

The income of the workers and staff should be gradually increased in coordination with increases in production and labor productivity. Wages in the lower brackets were raised by 30–60 percent during the three-year period of economic rehabilitation (1949–52), and the average pay of workers and staff rose by some 30 percent during the First Five-Year Plan period (1953–57). However, wages increased very slowly in the ensuing years and did not rise at all in the ten tumultuous years of the Cultural Revolution (1966–76). As a result, the average was essentially at the same level as that of two decades ago. This affected the enthusiasm of the workers and staff. After 1976 the government introduced some wage increases. In the past few years, the vast majority of workers and staff in the country have benefited from these increases.

The historical gaps between the living standards of the workers and the peasants should be narrowed gradually on the basis of better production. Due to the nature of agricultural production, the income of peasants is less than the generally low pay of industrial workers. If this difference remains too long, it will be harmful to a further consolidation of the worker-peasant alliance. China is gradually narrowing the gap by developing industrial, and especially agricultural, production and by improving living standards throughout the country.

The system of distribution according to work should be coupled with the establishment of better collective welfare facilities that will lighten the burden of household chores for workers and staff. At the present level of distribution in China, the working people operate within a tight budget. All governmental institutions and enterprises are encouraged to run good public dining halls, living quarters, nurseries, clinics, and other welfare facilities to ensure a worry-free work environment.

The forms of wages utilized under socialism are also very important. These forms include time wages and piece wages, supplemented by bonuses and job subsidies. Whatever forms are adopted, they should be conducive to the implementation of the principle of "to each according to his work." Bonuses are likewise necessary to encourage the workers; in particular, they are a necessary supplement to time wages.

CONCLUSIONS

Since the means of production belong to the whole people, the socialist state-owned enterprises should generally follow a unified wage scale on the principle of equal pay for equal work. But the situation is complicated by many factors.

From the very outset, wages in enterprises varied considerably from area to area and from trade to trade. Elimination of such differences is difficult as long as the two systems of socialist public ownership exist. The wages in small towns are much lower than those in big cities. When the government announced the national wage scale in 1953, it divided the country into ten zones, each separated by a 3 percent difference in pay. Small towns generally belonged to the first or second zones, where the wages were the lowest, and were later upgraded to the third or fourth zones. The large cities were placed in the sixth to eighth zones, while some border areas were rated as ninth or tenth. The classification was based mainly on the differences in the prices of food grain and nonstaple foods, which made up, as they do now, a large percentage of the means of subsistence of the workers and staff in

China. Being close to rural areas, people in small towns could get their food at fairly low prices. There were considerable difficulties impeding a strict application of the principle of equal pay to equal work among the workers and staff in different zones. This complicated situation in China has to be taken into account in any reform in the wage system or reclassification of the wage zones if the income gap between workers and peasants is to be kept within a certain limit.

Wages vary from one trade to another in the same area. They are generally higher in industry than in commerce, in heavy industry than in light industry, and in light industry than in the handicrafts. This shows that the application of a unitary pay scale is difficult even among state-owned enterprises. With its large population, China cannot solve the employment problem unless it undertakes a simultaneous development of enterprises of all sizes and of mechanized, semimechanized, and handicraft production.

A more serious drawback of the present wage system lies in the fact that all state enterprises follow the same pay scales irrespective of the fulfillment of their production quotas or contributions to the nation. This is another form of egalitarianism that is as harmful to socialist economic development as equal treatment for all, irrespective of quantity and quality of work. The principle of distribution under socialism should take into account both the contributions that workers make to their enterprises and the contributions enterprises make to the state. The workers and staff of an enterprise that makes outstanding contributions to the state should receive more pay bonuses and profits. Only then can the interests of the state, the enterprise, and the worker be combined properly. The egalitarian tendency to disregard the performances of the workers and staff has long since been criticized, and improvements have been made as the result of a reintroduction of piece wages and bonuses, and the effort should be kept up in future wage readjustments. Yet the egalitarian tendency to disregard the performances of enterprises has only just become a subject of discussion, and measures are being adopted to overcome it step by step.

Flexible methods should be adopted in wage reforms. As long as the total budgetary appropriation for wages is not exceeded, the localities and enterprises should be allowed much leeway in its distribution. The following recommendations may be considered: First, within the budgetary appropriation for the wages to be paid in an area, the local authorities may have the power to make proper adjustments in the wage rates in the trades and enterprises under their administration. Second, acting within the scope of wage appropriation, an enterprise may have the power to work out its wage rates and bonuses, subject to approval by the workers' congress of the enterprise and by the authorities in charge of the enterprise. Third, an enterprise may have the power to set aside part of the wage funds it saved by raising labor productivity and cutting down the labor forces and to use it for pay raises.

The authorities in charge of wages and labor forces in China have exercised a control over wages that is far too wide and rigid. To overcome egalitarian tendencies that had prevailed for many years, the state allocated a considerable sum of bonus money in 1978. But as the bonuses were to be distributed by a fixed percentage for each grade and were actually divided into equal shares in many areas and enterprises, they gave almost no encouragement to the better workers. From now on, the choice of candidates for pay raises and recipients of bonuses should be based on the principle of rewarding the advanced and spurring on those who lag behind. There should be more pay raises and bonuses for advanced enterprises, workshops, teams, and individuals and fewer or even none for the lagging ones.

4

Chinese Economic Reforms

Shortly after the founding of the People's Republic of China, many private enterprises were nationalized and converted into state-run enterprises. During the First Five-Year Plan, a central planning system, similar to the one in the Soviet Union, was developed and implemented. Large state-owned enterprises were placed under the control of central departments. All matters related to finance, materials, labor, production, supply, and distribution were centrally planned.

In its early years, the economy of the People's Republic was relatively simple, and central planning was effective because it allowed for proper mobilization of scarce resources such as capital and materials. However, as China's economy grew and became more complex, it became apparent that central planning was reducing the initiative of firms to improve. Thus, starting in the 1960s, there was a move in China, as well as in other socialist countries, toward economic reforms. These economic reforms sought to decentralize economic decision making.

This chapter discusses the major problems with central planning, identifies the need for reforms, explains the types of reforms needed, presents the economic reforms to date, and takes a look at potential future reforms.

MAJOR PROBLEMS WITH CENTRAL PLANNING

The highly centralized Soviet economic system served as a model for all the newly emerged socialist states. While this system played a positive role in the postwar or postliberation periods, allowing for quick economic rehabilitation and development and promoting the socialist transformation of the private ownership of the means of production, defects in the system became increasingly apparent after the basic completion of socialist transformation and the expansion in economic construction. Under the prereform model, once the plan targets had been fixed by the planning authorities, individual enterprises merely had to carry out the plan directives. Planning indicators such as gross output, assortment of goods, price, number of persons to be employed, and the total wage bill were fixed by the planning body. Raw materials and other immediate goods were also centrally allocated to individual enterprise. Problems of overcentralization and egalitarianism were frequently encountered.

Overcentralization

Industrial enterprises lacked sufficient power to handle their personnel and financial and material resources and also lacked guidance in their production, procurement of supplies, and the marketing of products. Productions and business operations were subjected to direct orders from administrative agencies, which controlled all the administrative measures. The enterprises provided them with all their means of production and bought up all their products. It took almost all their income and paid for all of their expenses. Thus, the enterprises were appendages of the administration. This put the enterprise in a passive position, fettering the initiative and creativity of both the enterprise managers and the workers. As a result, producers often overlooked the needs of consumers, with some products chronically in short supply and others overstocked, resulting in enormous wastage.

Egalitarianism

Egalitarianism has been a big problem, particularly in the Chinese case. In emphasizing mass equality, called "eating from the same big pot" in China, worker productivity and cost efficiency were ignored, with workers all paid almost equal wages. Such a practice, which seemed to foster equality, in fact promoted inefficiency, laziness, and general apathy toward work. A basic principle of socialism is distribution according to work. Egalitariansim dampens workers' initiative and hinders the growth in production.

These problems with central planning indicated that economic reforms, methodically implemented, were essential for China's continued economic development.

THE NEED FOR REFORMS

The present system of economic management in China is highly centralized, relying primarily on administrative methods of management. It was basically copied from the Soviet Union during the latter period of Stalin's leadership. China's experience over the past 35 years has revealed many defects in this model. These can be summed up in four separate aspects.

Enterprises have become mere appendages of administrative organs at different levels, and their relative independence has been negated. These enterprises lack initiatives and are treated almost as beads on an abacus that can be moved to and fro by the central ministries and the administrative organs of the localities. It is not that the enterprises do not wish to have initiative, but rather the system restricts their initiative.

Because the government manages the economy through administrative systems and divisions, the intrinsic relations within the economy have been cut off. For example, the enterprises are administered by the responsible governmental organs at the central or local levels, resulting in a predominance of vertical relationships and few horizontal relationships. This has been the cause of much irrationality.

In the economic plan, there are too many targets that are rigidly set by the higher authorities and handed down in the form of directives, so that producers and consumers do not contact each other directly. Production is not coordinated with marketing and is divorced from the needs of the consumers. As a result, there is overstocking of many products that cannot be sold, while many other products that are in great demand are always in short supply.

The enterprises have to turn over all revenues to the state, and losses are subsidized by the state. Thus, the enterprises do not feel any economic responsibility and do not pay attention to economic results. As a result, egalitarianism is prevalent among the employees of enterprises, since they are assured of their "iron rice bowls" and can "eat from the same big pot."

Due to these defects, the economic structure is wholly ineffective in mobilizing the enthusiasm and creativity of enterprises' workers and staff members. Besides, it is detrimental to the goal of achieving modernization and to the effective management of Chinese economy. Under such a system, practically everything is included in a unified plan of the national economy, with the state having a monopoly on purchasing and marketing commodities. The state is also responsible for arranging jobs for the labor force. Finally, the state is in charge of all revenues and expenditures.

This heavy involvement on the part of the state requires a highly centralized form of management that relies mainly on administrative means, instead of economic ones. With such an economic structure and managerial methods, socialist commodity production cannot develop rapidly. The sluggishness of the economy and the poor economic results are very much related to defects in the present economic structure.

The reason that China has practiced this management style for such a long time has been due to the incorrect understanding of the nature of the socialist economy. In particular, China failed to consider the socialist economy as a planned economy in which commodity production and circulation exist. An essential characteristic of a socialist economy is a planned economy that is based on public ownership of the means of production. The regulatory role of the market acts as a supplement that is brought into play in order to actively develop commodity production and exchange.

DIFFERENCE BETWEEN THE NATURE OF
COMMODITY PRODUCTION IN SOCIALISM
AND CAPITALISM

Capitalist commodity production is established on the basis of private ownership and is not centrally planned; moreover, labor is considered to be a factor of production, which can lead to the existence of exploitative relations of production. A socialist economy, on the other hand, is established on the basis of public ownership of the means of production. Both commodity production and exchange are planned. But the question of commodity production under socialism has been a major subject of discussion for over a century and also a topic of debate among Marxists. In *Critique of the Gotha Programme*, written in 1875, Marx referred to socialism as the initial stage of communism with vestiges of the old society still remaining. By the phrase "vestige of the old society," Marx was referring mainly to the system of distribution of income according to work done. Marx at that time conceived of socialism as having no commodity or monetary relations because it would be established on the basis of a highly developed capitalist economy. Marx did not then foresee that countries with a moderate degree of capitalist development, or even a country such as China in which capitalism was only in its initial phase of development and the natural economy was still predominant, could also successfully carry out socialist revolution and build socialism. Socialist construction in an economically underdeveloped country requires that commodities and money be fully utilized. In other words, a socialist economy is a planned one that should actively develop commodity production and exchange.

In 1917 Lenin also advocated the abolition of commodities and money in a socialist society. After the victory of the October Revolution, the economic system known as war communism was adopted in the Soviet Union. It was related to the guiding theory of abolishing commodities and money. The attempt to abolish commodities and money during the period of war communism failed, and Lenin extracted the lessons of this experience. He put forward the New Economic Policy based on the fact that the Soviet Union's economy at that time was made up of five economic components, predominant among which was the small commodity economy and small-scale production. The New Economy Policy was aimed at utilizing commodity and monetary relations to develop commerce and promote the rehabilitation and development of the socialist economy.

However, Lenin passed away soon after transformation was completed under the leadership of Stalin, and only the socialist economic component remained. Under such conditions, should there still be commodity production and exchange?

After the completion of agricultural collectivization, Stalin pointed out that two kinds of public ownership existed side by side—that is, ownership by the whole people and collective ownership—and that two classes existed, the workers and peasants, hence the need for exchange. But for a very long time after the completion of agricultural collectivization, Stalin did not clearly explain or prove whether the change between these two kinds of public ownership was commodity exchange or whether the law of value played any role. As a result, these questions were debated throughout this period in the Soviet Union. It was not until 1952, in his later years, that Stalin recognized that relations of commodity production and exchange existed between these two kinds of public ownership; he also held that the law of value should be utilized. But he maintained that the means of production are not commodities under the socialist system. He also repeatedly emphasized that commodity production and the role of the law of value should be restricted. One can say, therefore, that Stalin never considered the socialist economy to be a planned economy in which socialist commodity production and exchange should be actively developed, but viewed it rather as a seminatural economy. In view of such a theory and understanding, the structure of economic management put into practice during his time was not designed to meet the requirements of the planned development of commodity production and exchange, but rather the requirements of a seminatural economy. The economic management system of the Soviet Union at that time did not treat products as commodities, nor was the principle of exchange at equal value implemented. What was implemented instead was a system of mandatory planning that completely excluded the regulatory role of the market, and a highly centralized system of management that principally relied on administrative methods. This system of planning by decree treated the national economy as if it were one big factory. But as things stand now, the economy is more complicated than a factory. It was found that viewing the whole national economy as one big factory gives rise to a multitude of problems. A highly centralized system of economic management has negated the relative independence of enterprises. The theory and practice of Stalin had a tremendous impact on China's socialist construction.

The system of economic management that has been implemented in China up to the present has basically been patterned after Stalin's model, though there have, of course, been some changes. A number of aspects have been mentioned, such as a virtually all-inclusive state economy plan, state monopoly in purchasing and marketing commodities, state responsibility for assignment of jobs, the state's responsibility over all revenues and expenditures, and the practice of "eating from the same pot"—all these are basically a part of Stalin's model. If China can change this model, it should break through the trammels of erroneous or outmoded ideas.

The Chinese have already achieved a theoretical breakthrough, and this should be considered a significant achievement. Without such a breakthrough, ideas about how to initiate reforming the system cannot be developed. The Chinese government has recognized that not only the means of livelihood, but also a large portion of the means of production, are commodities under socialism. Also, commodity exchanges occur both between state-owned enterprises and collectively owned establishments, and within the state-owned sectors.

TYPES OF REFORMS NEEDED

Economic reforms in China must proceed from the vantage point of a desire to develop China's productive forces. Furthermore, the characteristics of its socialist economy must be taken into consideration. The salient features of the Chinese economy are its massive land, gigantic population, weak industrial foundation, low productivity, backward technology, imbalance among economic sectors, underdeveloped commodity production, and poor transportation and communication facilities. Because of this state of affairs, the reforms should focus primarily on the development of

that part of the economy in which the state sector is to play a
dominant role while coexisting with the other sectors, which include collectively owned enterprises and the individual economy.
Nine major types of reforms can be identified.

First of all, in order to run such a system, economic planning
should be integrated with the market. That is, primary reliance
should be placed on the economic machinery and economic means
to serve genuinely the interests of the state, of the collectives, and
of the broad masses. For such a reform, an enterprise should be
free from rigid state control and be treated as an independent economic entity, which implies the responsibility for profits and losses.
Enterprises should carry out their activities according to both social needs and the guidelines laid down in state plans.

National, regional, and interregional economic organizations
should be set up according to the principles of the division of
labor and industrial interdependence. This will improve the shortcomings in the current economic system in which enterprises are
mutually exclusive, fragmented, and poorly coordinated.

China should expand the sector of commodity production and
circulation and establish a unified market in which capital goods
and consumer goods can be traded as commodities, except for a
few necessities that will continue to be rationed according to state
plans.

Economic and trade centers should be set up where activities
will be carried out according to intrinsic industrial interdependence, which is dictated by natural economic connections rather
than according to administrative functions or geographical distribution. In the past, Shanghai, Wuhan, Guangzhou, Chongqing,
and Shenyang served as natural economic centers. These centers
served as focal points for economic activity. However, their importance was diminished when economic activities were centrally
organized. Establishing economic and trade centers would lead to
a well-developed network for the circulation of goods.

China should reverse the existing planning practice that arbitrarily imposes production targets from the top and should replace
it with a planning system that integrates both the upper and the
lower levels. Mandatory directives should be tempered by flexible
guidelines.

Instead of relying on administrative control, China should use price, taxation, and monetary policy, as well as other means to regulate economic activities.

Work discipline should be strictly enforced, economic legislation strengthened, and supervision tightened.

The party and the state organs should be relieved of their routine functions so they can focus on policy. Operations and decision making should be left to the enterprises, with no party or state interference.

State control should be relaxed, and some of the economic power should be delegated to regions that under state-unified leadership are to be responsible for planning, implementing, and supervising economic activities. Factory management should be responsible to the workers' congress rather than to the factory party committee.

These factors constitute an organic whole. If and when they are incorporated and carried out in the reform, the economic system will encompass both the virtues of socialist planning and the merits of a market economy, for it will be primarily a centralized system and yet have no rigid control. Such a system can develop a socialist commodity economy and enhance the socialist productive forces.

ECONOMIC REFORMS TO DATE

China has implemented a number of economic reforms in recent years. In the Third Plenary Session of the Eleventh Central Committee of the Chinese Communist Party, convened in December 1978, the "four modernizations" policy was initiated. The reform began in the field of agriculture. The third plenum proposed a series of guidelines for changing the managerial system in the rural areas, including the following: respecting the property rights and decision-making powers of production teams; adhering to the principle of "to each according to his work;" restoring and protecting the commune members' private plots and household boundaries; reopening rural bazaars; and increasing state-purchasing prices for farm and other agricultural by-products.

This is followed by the development of a system of responsibility in agricultural production founded on the public ownership of the basic means of production, chiefly the land. The most common way of accomplishing this was by contracting for production with the individual household. While commune members maintain collective ownership and unified management, households or, in some cases, individuals, have responsibility for certain tasks and contract to produce a certain amount of the whole that goes to the commune to be sold to the state. Contracting with the household is now being done in many production teams where the collective economy is highly developed and the peasants' livelihood has already improved considerably. This system of responsibility in agricultural production is being introduced extensively and signifies a big change in the collectives in China's rural areas. The improvement in the organization of agricultural forces and in the methods of remuneration is an initial adjustment of the relations of production—there *is* a cure for the overconcentration and unitary forms of management and operation.

Reforms in the managerial system are also being tried in industry by focusing on the extension of the decision-making powers of the enterprises. The reforms have been tried out on a limited number of enterprises and will be widened with experience. Basically, these pilot enterprises no longer turn over all their profits to the state or rely on the state to cover their expenses or even losses. By retaining a portion of their profits, incentive is provided to the staffs and workers, making them more conscious of the level and effectiveness of management, the market conditions, and the quality of their work. In 1979 production in these industrial enterprises increased 11.6 percent as compared to the 7 percent in nonexperimental enterprises. The experiment brought about an increase in the income of the state, the enterprises, the workers, and better goal congruence among all three parties.

In an expanded pilot experiment, decision-making power was delegated to many enterprises. Up to the first half of 1982, the experiment covered approximately 6,000 enterprises whose products accounted for 45 percent of the gross value of industrial product in the public sector of the economy. Having acquired new capacities of production and distribution, the enterprises began emerging as independent economic entities. According to the statistics of 84 local enterprises in Sichuan Province, the output value for 1984 rose 33 percent compared to an increase of 14.9 percent in 1979.

Since the reinstatement of the market under state guidelines, the means of production traded as commodities have gradually found their way to the market, and more channels have opened up for consumer goods. In the past, capital goods were produced and distributed according to state plan; now they are freely produced and marketed after the planned target has been fulfilled. For example, steel produced in 1979 over and above the planned target of 20 million tons was sold in the market. In 1979 alone, there were 600 new enterprises and 60 new trade centers that manufactured, marketed, and shipped capital goods for other enterprises. It is estimated that goods worth over 3.5 billion yuan were traded. These enterprises were even more active in producing and marketing consumer goods. According to the preliminary statistics, over 35 percent of the consumer goods were produced for and channeled through the market.

A new public finance system has been put into effect recently, according to which the state and the local government must delineate their respective revenues and expenditures, as well as their allocation of investment funds. This delineation of financial responsibilities between levels of administration, together with the profits retention incentive, have aroused the enthusiasm of both enterprises and local governments, cut down expenditures, and raised revenues. The favorable development stems from separating the financial management of the different levels of administration and from retrenching expenditures while augmenting revenues. Many local governments took the initiative and transformed or closed down enterprises that had long incurred losses. All these improvements have strengthened financial management and enhanced the reform.

Some enterprises have begun to specialize while maintaining coordination with various affiliated factories and with the head office. In keeping with the principle of the division of labor, a number of provinces and cities have formed specialized corporations and multifunctional enterprises. Statistics from 17 provinces and cities indicate that since 1979 over 1,000 specialized corporations have been established. This change has not only improved economic efficiency; it has also fully tapped the potentials of individual provinces or cities.

On a trial basis, capital construction will be financed by bank loans rather than by free state appropriation. Construction projects in the experiment include light industry, commerce, tourism, and so on. In the past, funds for capital construction were directly appropriated by the state, and neither the appropriating department nor the recipient department was responsible for profits or losses. As capital funds were freed, local government and enterprises used to compete for more funds, but they paid little attention to economizing in using the capital. Now, since investments are financed by bank loans, capital efficiency has been enhanced, and enterprises that borrow from banks are subject to the latter's supervision and auditing. For instance, the Shanghai Nonferrous Rolling Metal Works, with a planned annual processing capacity of 10,000 tons of copper, applied for 6.85 million yuan to expand its capacity to 40,000 tons—the amount applied for was three times over actual need. When bank loans replaced free state appropriation, the steel mill manager, worrying about the cost of the loan, took merely 2 million yuan. The planned capacity was met by technical innovations and a better utilization of the existing facilities.

Multitrade models have been developed, and resources of different economic sectors have been pooled. Agricultural policy has been liberalized to suit the conditions of individual localities, especially the poor, remote mountainous areas where production quotas were formerly fixed down to the production team or even to the individual household. The individual private economic transaction is now permissible. Collectively owned handicrafts, retail stores, restaurants, repair shops, and transportation and construction teams have been revived in cities. Besides, the reinstatement of individual handicraft workers and peddlers created many jobs, enlivened the market, and improved the people's livelihood.

In short, although the experiment started just recently, it has already broken the shackles of the existing economic system, galvanized and stimulated the initiatives of people in many areas, and motivated enterprises and workers to improve management and increase production. It has achieved favorable economic results, revived the whole economy, and paved the way for further reform.

FUTURE PROBLEMS

A comprehensive overhaul of the economic management system is an intricate and complex task. Chinese and foreign experiences suggest that reforms can be carried out step by step only when the conditions are ripe. The current reform, which may last several years, should not be too hasty. There were extensive and far-reaching reforms in China in 1958 and 1970 respectively, but neither achieved satisfactory results. One of the reasons for the failures was a lack of preparation and planning. The old system had been cast away before the new one was fully planned, and thus it was hastily put into effect. History demonstrates that a successful reform calls for great resolution, clear direction, good coordination, and phased progress in the right sequence. At present, the economic reform in China has entered upon a crucial transition period. China should promptly set up the main objective of the reform and the means to achieve this objective and then persistently push the reform forward. The objectives of reform for the immediate future are explained below.

Improving the Initial Reforms

China shall continue to improve its initial reforms. A major issue is how to coordinate the new measures and to develop them even further. So far, the experiment has been confined to delegating decision-making power to the enterprises, primarily the power of disposing of a portion of the earned profits. From now on, an enterprise should be allowed to draft its own plan, market its product, and purchase materials and equipment, as well as to develop the restructured and reoriented enterprises in light of the reform policy. It is necessary to create jointly operated enterprises and to encourage trades such as handicrafts, restaurants, repair shops, and other services, whether under collective ownership or private ownership. Correspondingly, China should open up more channels of circulation for both capital and consumer goods according to market supply and demand. Some of these goods are under state uniform purchase and sale, some under planned trade, some under preferential treatment, and others are to be freely traded.

Pricing System

The prices of the means of production call for extensive read-justment. For example, some enterprises earned profits because of efficient management, but other profits were incurred as a result of irrational state pricing. To remove the cause of the unfair distribution of profits between enterprises and to encourage competition, a multitier price system may have to be placed in operation.

Once reform of the economic management system is started, especially after market regulation occurs, the existing deviation of prices from actual values will not last for long. Therefore, the question of how China should manage the relation between price stability and price adjustment is central in pricing reforms. China must expedite the formulation of a series of specific policies to ensure that, provided prices for major livelihood means are basically stable, prices for other products, especially producer goods, can be adjusted accordingly. The price adjustments should not be handled exclusively by price departments. Experience shows that this task cannot be handled by such departments alone.

In addition, it is felt that price stability is very hard to maintain. The overall movements of prices after adjustments may be upward. Fluctuations in prices depend mainly on production development and the balance between money supply and the social demand for money, that is, the balance between money supply and social supply of commodities. During the Second Five-Year Plan, the state's planned management of process was greatly strengthened, but, owing to the declining agricultural output since 1959 and the 40 percent increase in the money supply, prices of agricultural products shot up. As a result, the state had to control prices resolutely over 18 categories of major consumer goods. With the rise in agricultural output in 1962, prices in agricultural products fell back to normal.

Price adjustment is by no means an easy task. The deviation of prices from actual values has been accumulating for more than ten years. The extent of the needed price adjustment is very large. To a large degree, certain price adjustments will adversely affect the people's livelihood and the budgetary balance. Therefore, it is imperative that there must be a clear direction of price adjustments and that such adjustments must proceed gradually—starting with those that pose the least disruption to the people's livelihood and the budgetary balance.

Price adjustments of producer goods affect the national economy and the people's livelihood most and thus must be done very cautiously. For producer goods like coal or timber, the effects will be apparent in the production costs of most enterprises and most consumer goods. Coal is China's most important source of energy. Prices for coal in China are about 50 percent lower than the world market prices, and the coal industry, as a whole, manages only to cover costs or, at most, to turn in a marginal profit. Close to half of the coal mines experienced losses. It is imperative that prices of coal be raised. But the steps toward increasing prices must be carefully arranged in order to avoid massive requests for general price increases. For lumber the negotiated prices are so much higher than planned prices that lumber producers are reluctant to deliver their product to the state for unified allocation. Instead, they want to sell lumber on their own. If the government forbids negotiated transactions, China will have problems obtaining wood furniture, building materials, and packaging for export products. These problems must be carefully handled by phasing in price adjustments.

Fiscal Policy

Instead of continuing the current practice that requires enterprises to turn over their revenues to the state, China should systematically use profit taxes. This change will not only assure an enterprise a reasonable return on investment under normal conditions, but also provide the state and local governments with a steady and reliable flow of revenues.

Monetary Policy

While maintaining overall control, China should let banks finance an enterprise's capital investment, instead of the present direct allocation of construction funds and working capital by the state free of costs. In that case, banks would perform some functions of economic regulation.

Employment

With respect to employment, China should adopt every measure feasible to create jobs, including projects to be organized by labor unions or labor departments and by self-employed individuals. Within the framework of the state labor plan, enterprises should be allowed to hire and discharge employees freely and thus foster competition.

Strengthening State Planning

China should strengthen state planning. With the expansion of a horizontal coordination of economic activities, a mandatory fulfillment of planned targets, which represents the former vertical coordinator, will be reduced. Nevertheless, planning as a guide for economic activities will be strengthened, for to meet the demand of socialist large-scale production, to ensure proportional growth among various sectors of the economy, and to prevent anarchy in production and construction, it is necessary to stress state planning. The state should focus its attention primarily on important objects, such as attaining comprehensive and overall balance in long-range plans, setting priorities for major construction projects, defining the scope and scale of capital investment, maintaining adequate ratio among the different sectors of the economy, and raising the people's standard of living.

In drafting short-run annual plans, four principal balances should be stressed: state budget, material supplies, bank credit, and foreign exchange. Using various economic measures, the state should provide guidance to enterprises so that they can carry out their activities within the planned framework. Once a long-range plan is drawn up, individual enterprises can each work out an annual plan on a contractual basis, from low levels all the way to the top, striking a balance on every level and reaching out for vertical integration. This system will certainly lead to a better integration between economic planning and the market.

Strengthening Information System

Simultaneously, China should strengthen its statistical system, setting up information centers, creating data banks, and making accurate economic forecasts. Moreover, China should establish adequate machinery to improve the coordination of economic activities. All these aids are bound to strengthen, expand, and improve China's economic planning.

CONCLUSIONS

As far as economic reforms in China are concerned, a proper handling of the relationship between economic planning and the market mechanism is crucial to the managerial reform. To give full play to the supplementary role of the market as a regulator of the economy with the framework of a planned economy, some different forms of management will have to be adopted on the basis of the importance of different enterprises to the economy and people's life, the system of ownership, and the importance, variety, and specifications of their products.

Generally speaking, some key enterprises and major products that are vital to the economy should be carried out under mandatory state plan. Their output value accounts for the greater part of the GNP, but the types of goods are limited. This covers a great variety of small commodities that are made by a large number of small enterprises and individual producers, but their output value comprises only a small percentage of the GNP. It is impossible to include all these goods in the unified plans. Such a planning system will combine reform on the unified state guidance with the initiative of the enterprises. It will be different from both the rigid conventional system and the perfect market economy under capitalism.

Economic reform in China is an enormous task because of its large population, uneven economic development, and complicated situations. However, the Chinese people are engaged in socialist modernization through experimenting and reviewing their experiences. These reforms may develop their productive forces while maintaining the advantages of socialism.

5

Market Planning in China

Socialist countries typically hold the view that planning in a socialist economy is significantly distinct from the market-oriented planning in a capitalistic country. Even if socialist planners would accept the argument that the law of value prevails in a socialist economy, they would still deny the existence of market forces in a centrally planned economy.

Until a few years ago such was the typical thinking prevailing in China. It was common practice for state commercial departments to purchase the output of factories. These commercial departments also provided the usual marketing functions in distributing the products. Quite often, what was produced was not what was demanded by consumers, and vice versa. The net result was inefficiency in the production and distribution of goods. This chapter describes some of the problems that have been associated with nonmarket-based planning and some of the reforms and suggestions for reforms to incorporate the market into the planning process.

PROBLEMS WITH NONMARKET PLANNING

One major problem with nonmarket planning is the lack of co-ordination of production with demand. Pricing, allocation of investment funds, and desire for self-sufficiency on the part of enterprises are some of the other problems discussed in this section.

Mismatch of Demand and Production

Because of the emphasis on planning and the neglect of the market, the problems of what to produce and how to produce were arbitrarily determined by high state officials and imposed on the enterprises. Consequently, production generally was not geared to social needs. Generally, what was produced found little demand, and what had been in demand was not supplied. Moreover, most of the goods produced by the enterprises were regulated under the state system of unified procurement and marketing. In addition, the bulk of the means of production was also under state-unified supply and planned allocation. There was little co-ordination between consumers and producers and no direct face-to-face contact. As a result, producers had no idea what consumers needed, nor could consumers exert any influence on production. Therefore, the disparity between the planned targets and the actual needs could not be properly reflected in the market, and the long-standing disequilibrium among production, supply, and distribution could not be attained.

Planned Prices and Demand

Since there were no objective criteria to determine the value of a product, the planned prices of many products deviated from their values by a wide margin. Without a valid criterion to determine the value of a product—and thereby the profit—it would be difficult to evaluate the performance of an enterprise. The profits and losses brought about by irrational pricing cannot be used to assess economic results. In the past, market supply and demand were rarely taken into consideration in establishing prices.

When commodities fell short of demand, instead of adjusting prices to raise supply and discourage demand, the government issued coupons. Thus, coupons took over the functions of money and created a multivalue system. Some people refer to this as "planned supply" and regard it as a feature of a socialist economy. However, what is not immediately apparent is that the suppression of demand by coupons has nothing to do with socialism. Admittedly, under certain conditions, within a period of time a socialist economy can impose quotas or fix prices to regulate supply and demand. Such regulations, however, cannot stimulate the production of commodities that are in short supply. Rather, such regulations often further aggravate production, thus reducing the supply. So the suppression of demand using coupons cannot fundamentally restore the equilibrium between supply and demand; in fact, it can worsen it.

Allocation of Investment Funds

The role of the market was ignored not only in production and distribution, but also in the collection of revenues and the allocation of funds. In the past, practically all enterprise revenues, profits, and depreciation funds were turned over to the state. In return, the state gave the enterprises all fixed assets and working capital free of charge. The enterprises were not held to be economically responsible for the efficient utilization of the assets and funds. Since the enterprises were not responsible for the profits and losses, economic accounting became a mechanical bookkeeping and auditing procedure rather than a device that could be used to motivate people to increase productivity. Under this situation, despite repeated administrative directives and appeals, the enterprises and their employees made little effort to meet the consumers' demands by reducing costs, improving quality, and increasing the variety. Up to this date, it has not been possible to eliminate wastes and inaction.

Desire for Self-Sufficiency

The socialist economy is based on large-scale production, which involves many departments and regions. With the advent of science and technology, specialization of production is bound to take place in a socialist economy. However, due to the lack of concern for the market and due to the outmoded methods of production, enterprises were driven to self-sufficiency instead of specialization. As a result, the practice of "small and complete" and "large and complete" became commonplace in China. It could be argued that the enterprises were not to be blamed for such a state of affairs. That could be attributed to a host of external factors, for instance, the imbalances in production, supply, and distribution and the frequent performance failure of other enterprises. From the entire economy's viewpoint, the self-sufficiency tendency can be attributed to the neglect of the market.

MARKET-BASED PLANNING IN A SOCIALIST ECONOMY

It should be pointed out that the notion that planning and the market are irreconcilable in a socialist economy is totally groundless in theory as well as in practice. Indeed, a socialist economy based on public ownership is operated according to state plans, but that does not mean it must sever all its relations with the market. What the socialist economy opposes is anarchy—the characteristics of an economy based on private ownership.

What is incompatible with the market is not the planned economy but the natural economy. In the natural economy, there is no commodity-money relationship but a system of distribution in kind. This is one of the basic features of all economies in which production is carried out in a state of anarchy and isolation. Production relations in a market economy are built on the basis of a social division of labor and coordination. Whether the market economy will be spontaneous and anarchical depends on the system of ownership. With socialist public ownership, market production can be placed under the people's conscious control and serve the socialist planned economy. Inasmuch as market production is based on the socialist division of labor, one can say, at least on this point, that it is not incompatible with the socialist planned economy, which is built on socialized large-scale production. Rather, economic planning and market production have something in common. The socialist planned economy existing under the conditions of commodity production relations uses money as the medium of exchange. As such, it is incompatible with the natural economy and spontaneous economy, but not with the market production economy under the people's conscious control.

In the past, the reasons that some people stressed only planning and neglected the market can be attributed to two traditional misconceptions. One attempted to equate the market with spontaneous production, particularly with the anarchy under capitalism; the other confused the planned economy with the natural economy. Some people often used the former as an argument to oppose the market. Whoever spoke of utilizing the market mechanism was thus branded as "going capitalist." Under the protection of the two traditional misconceptions and misled by the catch phrase "resolutely upholding the socialist planned economy and opposing the capitalist market economy," many irregularities and malpractices, which had nothing to do with socialism per se, flourished.

The economy was managed by simple administrative directives instead of economic laws. Work was performed according to the subjective wishes of senior officials rather than according to objective laws. Paternalism replaced the rule of democracy. Feudalism and bureaucratic management, which might be workable for a natural economy, are not substitutes for scientific management in large-scale socialist production. In a country where 80 percent of the people are peasants and where commodity production is still underdeveloped, the concepts and practices of self-sufficiency are deeply rooted in its social fibres.

At the present stage, when collective and state systems of ownership coexist, the commodity-money productive relations are quite important for Chinese economic development, particularly when the bulk of production is in the collectively owned agricultural sector. The role of the commodity is inconsistent with the ownership of the whole people, for although the view may be able to explain how the coexistence of the commodity-money productive relations and the market is brought about by exogenous factors, it cannot explain why there are intrinsic factors in the ownership of the whole people that must give rise to the coexistence of the commodity-money productive relations and the market.

In Chinese economic circles, several views have prevailed that are actually derived from the above-mentioned "external factor theory." Those views include "facadism" and "substitutism." The former refers to the fact that the means of production distributed in the system of the ownership by the whole people are no longer commodities. The latter maintains that the law of value and the value-related economic leverages—such as price, profit, costs, interest, and so on—are no longer regulators but simply dispensable accounting tools.

The existence of commodity-money productive relations in the system of ownership by the whole people is believed to be determined by material interests that exist during the stage of socialism. Under the system of public ownership of the means of production, antagonism between the exploiter and the exploited has been eliminated. However, during the stage of socialism, labor has not yet become a spontaneous social obligation but is merely a means of subsistence. Since people differ in ability and contribution, there will be differences in material compensations.

The differences in material interests are manifested not only among people but also among enterprises in the same system of ownership by the whole people. When differences in production performances among enterprises are brought about not by external factors but by their subjective efforts, the material compensations to the enterprises and their managerial staff and workers should be different; otherwise, production will be impeded. Therefore, the economic relationships among various enterprises (which are independent entities in the system of ownership by the whole people) must observe the principles of trade and compensation on the basis of equal value.

Any disregard of the principle of trade and compensation on the basis of equal value is a denial of the people's differences in material interests. This specific role of material interest under socialism is the direct cause of the existence of commodity-money productive relations. Of course, material interests are based on the division of labor and socialized production. Such a commodity relationship, or market production relationship, derived from the role of material interest under socialism, is deeply entrenched in the differences between people's material interests. It is neither an objective reality nor an economic mechanism. Here one must realize that so-called direct social labor resulting from ownership by the whole people refers to relations between individual labor and social labor that are free of the handicaps of the spontaneous markets of private ownership. In fact, during the stage of socialism, exchange between laborers, as well as between enterprises, must observe the principle of trading on equal value; therefore, the direct social labor can only be realized through a planned market. In other words, a planned distribution and conservation of social labor cannot be realized through the market mechanism that manifests a specific material interest relation under socialism alone.

Clearly, the relationship between planning and the market under socialism is neither mutually exclusive nor completely integrated by external forces. Rather, it is an internal organic integration determined by the very nature of a socialist economy. If it is the integration of the people's material interests under ownership of the whole people that created the material conditions for planned management, then the above-mentioned differences in the people's material interests under socialism is precisely the objective condition by which the contradictions between planning and the market in a socialist economy can be synthesized.

UTILIZING THE MARKET MECHANISM IN CHINA

Development of commodity production and utilization of the market mechanism cannot be carried out independently of the commodity producers' economic activities in the market. Apart from enterprises under collective ownership, the primary component of the socialist market consists of enterprises under ownership by the whole people. These enterprises sell to, as well as purchase from, the market all kinds of means of production and of consumption. To exercise the market functions, enterprises under ownership by the whole people must have the *right to make economic decisions* and be treated as independent commodity producers. If enterprises under ownership by the whole people were deprived of all rights and responsibilities, it would be meaningless to say that they made use of the market mechanism. Therefore, the issue of utilizing the market is intimately associated with that of extending the enterprises' right of management.

Under socialism, the market mechanism must rely on the economic leverages and economic machinery—including price, costs, interest, and taxes, which are all related to the law of value—to tie an enterprise's performance to its material interests. This reliance is the essence of making use of economic means to run an economy. Should one fail to pay attention to the economic leverages and the material interests of the individuals and enterprises, and rely solely on administrative methods to run an economy, then there is no need for utilization of the market. Therefore, all these issues are closely related to the problem of *operating an economy by economic means*.

In short, to make use of market mechanism, it is necessary to link it with the extension of an enterprise's economic rights and with the employment of economic means to run the economy. All these requirements are for the purpose of achieving a rational allocation and effective utilization of materials, funds, and labor according to social needs. But how can the market mechanism— the extension of private enterprise's right of management—and the use of economic means allocate labor, materials, and funds?

Allocation of Resources So That Production Is Determined by Supply and Demand

What commodities shall an enterprise produce and in what quantities? What are the rules governing an enterprise's marketing of its products? Where do enterprises get their resources? The previously mentioned method of production and marketing often resulted in a misallocation between social production and social needs and in a failure to fulfill production goals. We know that the goal of socialist production is to meet social needs and that the problems of what to produce and how much are determined by social needs. This is the basic principle of a socialist economy. As a rule, the enterprises produce according to state plans and according to social needs, but in practice there are contradictions between the two, for the state plans can only reflect the needs of society in general, not in specifics. Nor can the state plans take into consideration the concrete conditions of every enterprise. Therefore, the quantity, quality, and variety of commodities to be produced by an enterprise should be determined by the specific market demand and the interests of enterprise instead of being confined exclusively to the targets set by the higher authorities.

Correspondingly, the practices that allow the commerce departments to purchase and market capital goods and consumer goods regardless of whether there is demand for them must be ended. Except for a few goods that are in short supply, all goods should be distributed by the market. Gradually, consumer goods are to be marketed by the producing enterprise directly in order to meet the demand, and the producers' goods are to be treated as commodities. Producers and state procurement agencies should have direct contact, and their transactions should be regulated by contracts rather than by administrative directives.

Strengthening the market mechanism to solve some of the production and marketing problems lies essentially in reducing costs and increasing variety, improving quality and augmenting quantity, in removing shortage and eliminating surplus, as well as in enhancing the producers' interests and consumers' rights.

Recent figures indicate that state-owned textile mills are purchasing about 20 percent of their raw materials from the open market, enterprises operating under collective ownership purchase about 70 percent of their raw materials on the open market, while the comparative figures for communes run as high as 95 percent.

Consider the example of the Hangzhou Silk Printing and Dyeing Mill. Its production was state planned and distributed. At a sales fair, its products were considered to be old fashioned in comparison with products by the Shaoxing Silk Printing Mill. As a result, the director at the Hangzhou mill conducted what can be considered market research and developed 170 new designs. Subsequently, the new products were well received in the marketplace.

Allocation of Resources According to Economic Results

Until recently, Chinese policy on the allocation of funds has been essentially based on the notion of a fixed supply of capital with little market regulation. Inadvertently, this situation tended to motivate enterprises to compete for resources, funds, and foreign exchange and impeded the enhancement of investment efficiency and undermined the practice of economic accounting. To rectify this state of affairs, the government must change the present system of unified allocation of funds. Let the enterprises be responsible for their own profits and losses, and allow the banks to provide loans.

One way in which an enterprise can be responsible for its profits and losses is to allow it to keep a portion of its earned profits for expanding production, raising the employees' pay, or improving the workers' fringe benefits. However, this retention would be not allowed until the enterprise has paid taxes, interests, and loans. During the transition, an enterprise that has fulfilled its financial obligations would be allowed to retain a portion of its earned profits, which could be used to enhance work incentives, to allow technical innovation, or to expand productive facilities. Using these retained profits together with the depreciation allowance and maintenance funds, the enterprise could thus innovate, renovate, and expand production.

To shift the policy from a free appropriation of funds to bank loans with compensation, the state would levy a rental tax on an enterprise's fixed assets, which have been purchased with state funds. Such a tax—compensation for using state capital—together with the retained profits would enable those enterprises that utilize their funds efficiently and operate their businesses successfully to earn profits and accumulate reserves and thus increase their material interests. The reformed system, if implemented, would motivate an enterprise and its employees to tap their potential and fully utilize capital funds.

When the practice of an enterprise's managing of its own finances is well established, we should consider how to let bank loans and the enterprises' retained profits gradually replace the state appropriations of construction funds and working capital. Obviously, the enterprise will be more prudent, more economic, and less cavalier in using the funds when it is responsible for its profits and losses than when the funds are appropriated free compensation. The enterprise would be permitted to retain a portion of its earned profits after having repaid the loan plus interest. In making loans for capital construction or working capital, the banks would exercise discretion in fixing the interest rates. At the same time, the banks would watch the results of investments and grant loans on a selective basis.

Placing Employment on a Competitive Basis

In the past, among the allocation of labor and financial and material resources, allocation of labor was furthest from the market mechanism. The allocation of laborers to various departments was meted out according to the state plan, but the simplistic approach was cumbersome and created numerous problems, for often an enterprise could not hire the worker it needed and the individual could not choose a job that suited his or her talents. Who would get what job was determined by government officials. Apparently, this system was not a rational way to use labor, raise enthusiasm, improve economic accounting, or achieve better operating results.

To eliminate the misallocation and misuse of labor, the person best suited for the job would be selected, and planned assignment would be integrated with free choice of employment. Within the limits set by state regulations, an enterprise would have the right to hire the applicant best suited for the job. Likewise, an enterprise would have the right to *reassign surplus laborers* to wherever they are needed. During the transition, the employees' living allowances would be drawn from social insurance funds, and workers would have the freedom to choose their own occupation whenever feasible.

Generally speaking, free choice of occupation by individuals would by no means be construed as free movement from one enterprise to another. As the founder of scientific socialism stated, the freedom of individuals is a precondition for all people's free development. During the stage of socialism, particularly when the productive forces are still underdeveloped, uncontrolled free choice of occupations is not feasible—as it is possible under communism. Nevertheless, socialism considers working an inherited privilege. Under the present condition of "to each according to his work," after the worker's family, directly or indirectly, pays the expenses of education and training, the worker would be granted, within limits, the right to choose his or her occupation. Clearly, limited freedom in choosing one's occupation does not imply undisciplined movements of laborers between enterprises and departments or between rural and urban areas. Regulations of labor movements would rely primarily on economic measures and ideological education rather than on administrative and legislative measures. For instance, to encourage workers to stay on a job, a bonus may be granted for seniority; to induce workers to emigrate to remote areas or to take hard jobs, living allowances or wage differentials would be adopted.

PRICING AND COMPETITION IN CHINA

We have dealt with the issue of using the market mechanism for commodity production, allocating resources and market goods, and making the best use of labor in the planned socialist economy of China. The use of the market mechanism to regulate economic activities involves two important factors: price and competition.

Price

The regulatory functions of the law of value in socialist production have long been denied in China. Some people who champion constant prices try to equate stable planned prices with long-range frozen prices, but ever-changing economic activities cause frequent variations in factors that affect prices. Any arbitrary freezing of prices will run counter to objective law, causing prices to drift further and further away from reality. For instance, change in labor productivity would change the value of products, and productivity is the basic factor that determines price. The rates of change in labor productivity change faster in industry than in agriculture.

The current disparity between the prices of industrial and agricultural products is not due entirely to historical factors. Since labor productivity rises faster in industry than in agriculture, the disparity between the two would widen if their prices were to continue to be determined in the same way. Another example is supply and demand, which are the major factors that affect commodity price. If prices were frozen, there would be no way that they could reflect change in supply and demand, which is the reason that the supply and demand of many products is out of equilibrium in China. The state subsidizes those products whose prices are set below costs. Although the maintenance of a stable price level for a period of time may assure steady production and consumption, it can be detrimental, if prolonged, to production, for price control can suppress the symptom but not the disease of disequilibrium between supply and demand. Only through an expansion of production can the equilibrium between supply and demand be restored.

In the past, China paid an exorbitant price to maintain price stability. Numerous coupons and queues brought nothing but forced equilibrium at the cost of lowering the standard of living. Whenever a commodity is rationed or put under state control, its supply falls even more than if there were no ration. Rations dampen the incentive to increase production. Massive evidence has verified the fact that when the prices are irrational it is difficult to fulfill planned targets. At present, the prices of many commodities have drifted further and further away from their value. These disparities have already adversely affected Chinese economic development, particularly in agriculture, raw materials, and fuel.

To improve the situation in light of the spirit of the Third Plenary Session of the Eleventh Central Committee, price disparities between agriculture and industry have been narrowed, the relative prices of some major products have been adjusted, and enterprises are allowed to vary within limits of the planned prices. The critical question is whether China admits that price is a means of market regulation. If prices are allowed to fluctuate within a certain range, then supply and demand can perform the regulatory functions, thus stimulating production. This is precisely how the market mechanism would function under state guidance. Of course, allowing price variations would not be construed as condoning anarchy. In fact, price variations would not be allowed to deviate from the planned range. Consumer goods, which are essential to the masses, and the means of production would be put under state control for a limited period of time.

Competition

As long as a commodity economy prevails, there is competition. To a certain extent, competition and free price movement are interrelated and interdependent, together constituting an organic block of the market mechanism. Without price differentials, there is no competition; conversely, without competition, there are no price variations, no market regulations, and no operation of the law of value. That production and marketing should be carried out according to investment returns and that workers should be hired according to their abilities all hinge on competition.

Usually, people tend to link competition with capitalism, but, in fact, competition is not confined exclusively to capitalism. Rather, it is a characteristic that exists in all commodity economies. Since commodity production and commodity trade do exist under socialism, precluding competition would be tantamount to denying the existence of the commodity economy. Enterprises under socialism would operate as commodity producers, for whether the labor involved in its production is above or below the socially necessary norm will affect the material interests of people concerned. Competition between enterprises would certainly stimulate technology innovation, improve management, reduce costs, raise productivity, increase variety, and enhance quality. So competition will test an enterprise's efficiency and press an enterprise to satisfy the consumers' demand for better goods and greater variety, thus fostering the development of the productive forces.

It should be recognized that there are fundamental differences between competition under socialism and competition under capitalism. One of the basic differences is that competition in the former case is based on public ownership, in which the enterprises share common interests, while competition in the latter case is based on private ownership, in which the enterprises have conflicting interests. Since socialist competition is not between enterprises whose goals are mutually exclusive, it will not lead to anarchy or polarization between the rich and poor.

There are differences as well as similarities between what is called "socialist emulation" and capital competition. The similarities lie in that they both tend to push the laggard to catch up with the advanced and to exhort the advanced to make further advancement. Socialist emulation, however, does not involve material incentive nor the elimination of faltering enterprises, whereas capitalist competition is closely related to material interest, and even to the survival of an enterprise. To minimize social losses, the enterprises that cannot produce commodities to meet the market demand, or that incur losses because of factors beyond their control, would suspend operation or be converted to another product. More than that, the state would investigate who is responsible for losses, and the labor departments would find jobs for the laid-off workers. Unlike capitalism, there is no involuntary unemployment when an enterprise goes out of business.

Overall, the market can plan an active and broad role in a socialist planned economy—in production as well as in marketing, in the appropriation of funds as well as in the allocation of labor. The market mechanism can work well in these and other areas. To do so, however, it is necessary to confine price variation within the planned range. A flexible price, when properly set, is conducive to the realization of plan targets and to a rational and effective use of resources.

CONCLUDING REMARKS

In the course of building China's socialist economy, the market mechanism has long been ignored. There is a tendency to deny the usefulness of the market as a means to develop the socialist planned economy. Such a view is a fallacy that, if left unexposed, will prevent the market from playing a positive role and will hinder the integration of economic planning and the market. Moreover, another tendency to be opposed is to exaggerate the functions of the market at the expense of planning. This tendency seems to have appeared in China and abroad. For instance, some people equate planned economy with contempt. At this juncture, when China is reexamining the role of the market in socialist economy, it must guard against such tendencies.

China is striving to develop socialist commodity production by using the market mechanism. After all, the Chinese economy is not based on laissez-faire, and it cannot let Adam Smith's "invisible hand" sway its socialist system. On the other hand, material interest in a socialist economy consists of not just those of the individual but also those of given sectors. Only under state regulation can the interests of all sectors be properly integrated. The development of a socialist economy, therefore, calls for both planning and the market. For instance, a consumer's choice based on his or her preference, or production based on a single enterprise's decision, may or may not coincide with the overall social interest. If those decisions were made by the market forces alone, they might not result in an optimal and rational allocation of labor, funds, and resources. Nor would they necessarily conform to the requirements of social development.

In the course of rapid socialist industrialization and modernization, the industrial structure and the productive forces are often subject to sudden sharp changes. If every decision is made according to the market mechanism, the productive forces and the industrial structure could not be adjusted promptly. In developing a socialist economy, all such problems of strategic importance cannot be solved by the market mechanism alone but must be regulated by state and social planning. It is conceivable that an overreliance on the market rather than on state planning may distort the productive structure, particularly in remote frontiers and backward areas.

Another example may be of value. In a socialist economy, because of variations in material conditions (such as natural endowments, locations, and equipment), income distributions may differ among regions. If not redressed by the state, this gap in income distribution would widen, thus defying the very principle of socialism.

In a broad sense, socialism opposes both egalitarianism and excessively skewed distribution of income. While opposing egalitarianism, some differentials in income during certain phases of economic development can be tolerated to allow some people to earn more now so as to create the conditions that eventually will make all prosperous. Clearly, the regulation of income, which may sometimes narrow the gap and other times widen the gap, has to be carried out by economic planning and the market.

In short, to coordinate the activities of various departments and regions, to look after the interests of the whole economy, and to correctly handle the material interests of all sectors, it is necessary to intensify state planning while making good use of the market mechanism. Some people believe that economic planning and the market are complementary. Allegorically, one may compare decision making from a planned viewpoint with looking at things from a commanding vantage point and decision making from a market viewpoint with looking at things from the bottom of a deep ravine. Whereas the former may provide a macroscopic view but not much detail, the latter may present a microscopic view but not an overall picture. In a sense, this comparison is true, for state decisions are made in the interests of the whole economy, while consumer and enterprise decisions are made in the interest of the individual. The principle of socialism is to promote the interests of a whole economy, and consumer and enterprise decisions are made in the interest of the individual. The principle of socialism is also to promote the welfare of the whole society, including the state, the collectives, and the individuals. Hence, economic planning and the market must be integrated to harmonize those interests.

Can the national economy be strengthened by unified planning? The answer depends on what a planned economy is. In the past, people generally held the view that a genuine socialist planned economy is one in which high authorities set production targets. Thus, unified planning was equated with centralized leadership. The state directly controlled all enterprises, and the ministries and departments of the central government made decisions for the enterprises and the local governments. Ostensibly, this policy is detrimental to economic development. At the Third Plenary Session of the Eleventh Central Committee, a resolution was adopted that criticized the overcentralization of the state in managing enterprise. The characteristics of a socialist economy consist not so much of centralizing all labor and resources in the hands of the state but of coordinating all economic activities according to scientific forecasts. It would be a misconception for people to look upon the existence of a commanding state planning and a centralization of labor and resources as the cornerstone of socialist management. Then how can China strengthen economic planning by providing guidelines?

The Chinese perspective is that long-range programs, particularly five-year plans, which will set goals for major economic development, fix ratios between accumulation and consumption, allocate funds for capital construction and key projects, and improve the people's standard of living, should be drafted. Targets in the five-year plans may be broken down into annual rates, so they can be adjusted and revised if necessary. The state should focus on formulating policies and implementing plans.

Next, the mandatory section of the plan, which the enterprises must fulfill, would be gradually reduced until all planned targets become merely guidelines for economic activities. The state plans would forecast the trends of economic development so that enterprises and local governments can coordinate their activities accordingly. In light of the guidelines provided by the state and the market, every enterprise would draw its own plan. Here, it is clear that state planning plays a significant role, for if an enterprise had little idea of what the trend of the economy would be, it would have to draw its production plans according to the market situation alone. But state forecasts can provide the enterprise with accurate information of the market trend. The more scientifically the state plans are drawn and the more the plans conform to reality, the better the enterprise's policy will be and the greater the possibilities of fulfilling the planned targets. Conversely, if the plans were drawn by wishful thinking or by command from the top, they would still be taken seriously, but the results would not necessarily be desirable.

The reform, in fact, will enhance the work and the responsibilities of the state planning commissions. Now more than ever, these commissions are expected to produce scientifically drawn plans that can provide reliable information, which enterprises can use to carry out their activities.

To improve efficiency and to enhance the prestige of state planning, an enterprise's plan must be drawn independently, unit by unit and level by level, and the vertical integration of plans should start from the bottom unit, not the other way around. Problems concerning production, marketing, and the allocation of funds and other resources should not be submitted to the state if they can be solved by the market forces or by contract. This policy will not only spare the enterprise unnecessary interference, but also relieve the state of routine chores so that the state can focus on vital issues concerning the entire economy.

To ensure coordination in developing social production and fulfilling planned targets, economic policies would be formulated so that they serve as a guide for all economic activities, including price, tax, credit investment, income distribution, foreign trade, foreign exchange, and so forth. In pursuing these policies, the state would encourage those activities that are needed and restrict those that are redundant and thus help enterprises fulfill the planned targets. For example, to overcome the underdeveloped state of the fuel industry, the state would speed up its development by granting it tax rebates, price concessions, and favorable credit terms.

6

Pricing Mechanism
in China

Shortly after the formation of the People's Republic of China on October 1, 1949, the government started to undertake strong measures to control and stabilize market prices, to control inflation, and to adjust market prices within the context of social economic planning. By the beginning of the First Five-Year Plan in 1953, prices of major industrial and agricultural products were being set by the government rather than by the general action of demand and supply in the marketplace.

Given that the government sets prices, Western business persons quite often have the impression that these prices are not set objectively. Such, however, is not the case. The "law of value" is utilized quite extensively in socialist economies in setting prices for goods. The first section of this chapter examines the concept of the law of value. The second section contains an explanation of how the pricing system in China evolved over time. More recently, as China has undertaken economic reforms, it has had to cope with a number of problems in reforming the pricing system. These problems are discussed in the third section. The following section examines alternative price adjustment mechanisms. The chapter concludes with a discussion on reforming the pricing system.

THE LAW OF VALUE

The law of value says that commodities must be exchanged at their values, which are determined by the amount of socially necessary labor time spent on production of the commodities. In the rare situation when demand and supply are in balance, prices of the commodities will equal their values. More often, though, demand and supply are not in balance, leading prices to vary from the values of the commodities being traded. This usual variance between prices and values does not invalidate the law of value. Consider the case where demand exceeds supply. Prices rise above values. These price increases stimulate production. Increased production results in excess supply, forcing prices down. Value, then, can be understood as a trend or central value around which price fluctuates continuously.

In a capitalistic economy, changes in demand and supply create, and are reciprocally affected by, price fluctuations. These price fluctuations result in continual redistribution of labor and capital in the different sections of the economy.

In a socialist economy, the people own the means of production, and output is established by government plans. Prices for the goods produced are set by the government through utilizing the law of value. This law serves a very valuable role in a socialist economy in regulating output. Price fluctuations affect the economic well-being of both buyers and sellers. By using the law of value, the state can achieve a socially desirable balance between national income distribution to the state, the collectives, the peasants, and the workers.

EVOLUTION OF THE PRICING SYSTEM

China's pricing system has undergone a complex evolution in the past 35 years. Shortly after the formation of the People's Republic of China, the state began to set prices for major industrial and agricultural products. But because of the coexistence of several components in the economy, the state had to follow correctly the law of value in setting prices. When the state placed orders with capitalist industries, it not only had to calculate costs accurately, but also allow a reasonable profit for the capitalists. When the state purchased agricultural products from peasants, it not only had to generate a reasonable labor return to peasants, but also regulate the output of various agricultural products by adjusting prices. The state did a good job in combining planned regulation with market regulation until the socialist transformation of ownership in the means of production was completed. During the three-year recovery period (1949–52), market regulation predominated. However, state planning gradually strengthened its guiding role. In the First Five-Year Plan, with the development of the socialist state economy, the emphasis was gradually shifted to planned regulation. But since the capitalist economy and the individual economy still existed widely, market regulation continued to play an important role. Therefore, state planned prices were basically in line with the law of value. Product prices changed constantly with changes in production costs and conditions of supply and demand. At that time, the state's price policy was mainly to stabilize prices. Apart from reducing the price differentials between industrial and agricultural products, the question of price adjustment was not yet raised.

After the socialist transformation was completed, the state adopted the method of unified revenues and unified expenditures for the state industry. Because enterprises did not need to worry about their profits or losses, they were not concerned whether prices were high or low. The state adopted the methods of in-kind tax, unified purchase, and quota purchase toward major agricultural products. With "plan coming first, and prices coming second," prices increasingly deviated from values. Although the state raised the purchase prices for agricultural products many times, and adjusted prices for industrial products somewhat, price adjustment lagged far behind changes in objective conditions. Generally, because of limitations imposed by natural conditions, costs for agricultural products and mining products seldom decline with higher output. On the contrary, they may even rise. Costs for manufactured products, on the other hand, decline with higher output. As these trends continue, profit for the former products will be very low or negative, while profit for the latter products will be very high. Prices for both types of products deviate more and more from their values, producing what is known as the "scissors effect." Reasonable adjustment is therefore necessary.

In the three years of the "Great Leap Forward," the national economy suffered from a proportional imbalance, resulting in a decrease in agricultural output. With a rapid growth of the money supply, prices increased dramatically. In 1962, when the National Price Commission was established, it was decided that prices needed to be stabilized to control inflation. The commission set forth the policy of stabilization first and adjustment second. In the next two to three years, prices were basically stable, with some declines. A five-year plan to adjust prices was announced in 1965 and 1966. The policy was to raise prices gradually for agricultural products and some mining products. There were to be rises and falls in prices for light industrial products, with no overly upward or downward movements. Prices for some heavy industrial products were to be gradually lowered. The Cultural Revolution started almost as soon as the plan was implemented. For fear of disrupting the market, prices were temporarily frozen. In the next 12 years, prices remained basically unchanged, but the deviation of price from values continued to worsen. As a result, agriculture, mining, and some raw materials industries were often unable to fulfill their production targets, while the manufacturing industry, especially the machine-building industry, overfulfilled plans. Of course, unreasonable prices were not the major reason for the proportional imbalance in the national economy that was gradually formed over ten years. It was, however, one important reason.

In restrospect, it becomes apparent that the direction of the five-year adjustment plan put forth in 1956 was correct. But it could not have thoroughly solved the price problem. First, the degree of price of adjustment was too small, it could not have prevented the price differentials between agricultural products and industrial products; that is, the scissors effect could not have been reduced. It also could not rapidly realize the exchange of equal values between industrial and agricultural products or among industrial products. Second, there were hundreds of thousands of varieties of industrial products with up to a million different prices. If market regulation were not used, the price departments alone would surely have been unable to do a good regulation job. But if market regulation were to be used, the problem of reforming the whole economic management system would have to be faced. Consequently, reform of the price system was delayed for more than ten years.

RECENT PROBLEMS IN REFORMING THE PRICING SYSTEM

The first measure adopted to reform the price system was to raise substantially the purchase prices of agricultural products. The state continued to increase wages of staff and workers and resumed payment of bonuses. A 20-year debt to the people's livelihood was beginning to be repaid. At the same time, the government decided to reduce investment in capital construction and change the unreasonable proportional relation between accumulation and consumption. Of course, it was not possible to repay completely a 20-year-old debt to the people's livelihood in a few years. But in the meantime, a new problem had emerged: the growth rate of the people's income greatly exceeded the growth rate of the national output. The planned increase of the consumption fund was overachieved, and the planned reduction of the accumulation fund was underfulfilled, leading to a budgetary and credit imbalance. This newly created social purchasing power destabilized prices in the market. To counter this problem, the government was forced to stabilize prices resolutely, creating difficulties in the planning and adjusting of prices.

While adjusting the national economic proportions, the state started to implement reform of the economic management system. It combined planned regulation with market regulation by fully exploiting the regulating functions of the market under the direction of the state plan. Market regulation is, in fact, regulation through the use of the law of value. Under the condition when price deviates from values, current prices conflict with those determined under market regulation. One is thus forced to accelerate price adjustment. China's practical experience with institutional reform in the past few years has shown that if prices are not adjusted many unreasonable problems will be encountered in institutional reform. The major ones are explained below.

Unequal Distribution of Benefits and Costs

Profit retention is used to expand the autonomy of enterprises to encourage them to increase output, practice economy, and improve their performance in operations and management. This is undoubtedly a very good method. But as the prices of many products deviate substantially from their values, the size of enterprise profit does not depend mainly on operations and management, but rather on prices. Because prices are higher than values for products from some enterprises and lower than values for products from other enterprises, profit retention results in extremely uneven distribution of benefits and costs among enterprises. Thus, prices should be adjusted first before profit retention is implemented. Price adjustment is, however, a complex task requiring gradual adjustments. To reduce uneven distribution of benefits and costs, the proportion of retained profit is tied to the size of the enterprise profit. But once this method is adopted, it creates obstacles to later price adjustment. If prices are raised, enterprises get more profit, which makes the fiscal departments dissatisfied. If prices are lowered, enterprises get less profit, which makes them disgruntled. To change prices, the proportions of retained profit must be changed, leading to many disputes.

Coordination between Production and Marketing

In the past, many products were subject to unified purchase and guaranteed marketing. The great wall separating producing units and market needs led to chronic overstocking of many products and chronic shortages of many other products. Economic returns from production were greatly reduced as a result. Recently, market regulation was adopted for some products. Some commerce departments were allowed to purchase selectively according to market needs, and what was not purchased could be sold by plants independently.

Industrial and commerce departments all must adjust their production, purchases, and marketing according to market needs. But many abundant products command high prices and large profits. Their output still cannot be reduced. Many scarce products command low prices and small profits. Nobody is willing to produce them. In adopting market regulation, the state has to follow the law of value. Prices for abundant products should be allowed to fall, and prices for scarce products should be allowed to rise. If price departments do not actively make adjustments and do not allow the law of value to assist in making adjustments, great obstacles will be created for balancing the proportional relations among the various sectors of the national economy. This situation is even more serious in the allocation of the means of production, because of overly strict controls.

Since market regulation was started, some planned prices have been suspended. For example, in order to organize coordination through specialization in the machine-building industrial departments, profits among enterprises have to be adjusted. Coordination prices are set to supplant planned prices within and among some regions. Some coordination prices are higher than planned prices, while others are lower. Apparently, coordination prices are more in line with the law of value than planned prices. Negotiated buying and selling prices are used to market allocated producer goods. Some negotiated prices are markedly higher than planned prices, but there is nothing concrete that can be done about it. Only by raising planned prices and rewarding higher output (such as some minor steel products) will negotiated prices come down. For more chronically overstocked products, material resources departments should not only allow unrestricted supply, but also set discount prices, or producing units will not reduce output on their own initiatives. In some big cities, markets for agricultural and sideline products have recently opened, greatly increasing the supply of products. Some products are purchased and marketed by negotiation through supply and marketing cooperatives and warehouses. Their prices are inevitably higher than state prices. The opening of urban markets today is different from the past. At present, market prices are only slightly higher than planned prices (in some areas, prices for food grain are even lower than the incentive prices). In some areas, prices for meat and eggs are lower than planned prices, forcing state commerce to reduce prices to increase sales. It is to be expected that such negotiation transactions inevitably lead to some speculation and manipulation. Management must therefore be strengthened. But strict control should not be imposed. Too strict a control will not be conducive to developing production and improving living standards.

In short, once reform of the economic management system is started, especially after market regulation is adopted, the existing deviation of prices from values will not exist for long. Therefore, how to handle the relation between price stability and price adjustment once again becomes an issue of concern in price work. The state is moving to formulate a series of specific policies to ensure that, provided prices for major livelihood means are basically stable, prices for other products, especially producer goods, can be adjusted upward or downward to resolve the above-mentioned conflicts. The price adjustments need not be handled exclusively by price departments; practice shows that this is a task impossible for them to do alone. If the state is going to apply market regulation, it must be good at using the law of value to make prices of products gradually approach their values. Therefore, in adjusting prices, price departments should not concentrate on calculations but must seriously study problems relating to goals and policies. They must study how to use the law of value so that market regulation can facilitate the balance between supply and demand and not aggravate the imbalance.

ALTERNATIVE PRICE ADJUSTMENT PROPOSALS

Generally speaking, there is a conflict between price stability and price adjustment. If prices are adjusted upward and downward, the overall direction may be more upward than downward. In addition, it is felt that price stability is very hard to maintain. However, the actual situation is quite different. Fluctuations in prices depend mainly on production development and the balance between money supply and social demand or money—that is, the balance between social purchasing power and social supply of commodities. During the First Five-Year Plan, although the state still could not exercise strictly planned management because of the coexistence of several economic components, prices were basically stable since the money supply was carefully controlled. During the Second Five-Year Plan, the state's planned management of prices was greatly strengthened because the socialist transformation was completed. But, owing to the beginning of the decline of agricultural output in 1959, and the money supply's increase by 1.4 times between 1957 and 1961, prices in farmers' markets increased dramatically. Prices for minor commodities over which the state did not exercise complete control also rose. To protect the livelihood of its citizens, the state resolutely stabilized prices for 18 categories of major consumer goods. But it also had to sell some high-priced commodities to withdraw some money from circulation. With agricultural output starting to rise in 1962, prices in farmers' markets fell back to their normal levels. Practice shows that provided that output rises, especially when money supply does not increase excessively, prices can be basically stabilized.

At present, the money supply has not yet increased to the same extent as it did in the 1960s. At the same time, with bumper harvests in agriculture, prices in farmers' markets have not increased. But because prices for many products deviate markedly from their values, coordination prices begin to appear in the machine-building industry. Coordination prices for many extra-plan products that are produced in small local plants with high costs often exceed planned prices. For many scarce raw materials (such as steel and lumber) and agricultural sideline products with low planned prices, negotiated buying and selling prices are used to stimulate production and satisfy the needs of the people's livelihood. If the state is to use market regulation, it should not interfere excessively with coordination prices, negotiated buying and selling prices, and other internal prices. The best that can be done is to channel them in the right direction.

The present planned prices are actually far from stable. If they are not adjusted, it is possible that producing units may not try to complete planned allocation assignments, but may sell their products at negotiated prices. Therefore, the price level cannot remain stable if prices for many products consistently and substantially deviate from their values. A few years ago, the prices of certain agricultural products were raised in a planned way. The price level increased by 5.8 percent. As a result of chain reactions, the actual increase might have been higher. In addition, the budget was out of balance and money supply increased a little too fast. To some extent, these affected price stability. But price fluctuations today are different from those in the past. Because of the recent adjustments, prices are basically stable. Therefore, it is much easier to stabilize prices now than in the past. The state should not be afraid of necessary and possible price adjustments for the sake of price stability. Of course, present price adjustment is by no means an easy task. Because the deviation of prices from values has been increasing for more than ten years, it poses serious obstacles to the economy. The extent of the needed price adjustment is very large. Some price adjustments will adversely affect people's livelihood and the budgetary balance. Therefore, once the clear direction of price adjustments has been established, the state needs to proceed gradually, starting from those that pose the least disruption of the people's livelihood and budgetary balance.

Price Adjustments for Industrial Goods

There is a pressing need to adjust prices for industrial goods, such as machine products and steel products. Fortunately, such prices can be adjusted readily. These are problems that urgently need to be resolved if the production of industrial goods is to be increased. In the past few years, supply of machine products generally exceeded demand because of retrenchment in capital construction. Also, because prices were generally high and profits were comparatively large in this industry, using the law of value as a regulator may result in more price decreases than price increases, so that price stability will not be affected. Enterprises should be encouraged to negotiate coordination prices among themselves. These prices will facilitate adjustment of planned prices in the future. From 1983 to 1985, the inventory of steel products increased remarkably, and reducing this inventory is necessary. Abundant products that have been overstocked for years should be sold at a discount. At the same time, prices for some scarce products should be increased appropriately. To do this, enterprises should be allowed to negotiate buying and selling prices and actively adjust planned prices with reference to these prices so as to reduce overstocked inventory and encourage production of scarce products. At the same time, it is also necessary to change the method of setting prices for imported material resources in order to avoid conflicts with domestic prices. At present, prices for some imported commodities are fixed below domestic factory prices through subsidies by the Ministry of Foreign Trade. This is an unreasonable practice. The ministry should be allowed to reduce or eliminate subsidies so as to reduce imports and protect domestic production.

The above-mentioned upward and downward price adjustment need not adversely affect people's livelihood and price stability. Nor need they seriously affect fiscal revenues. However, every item of price adjustment affects the distribution of profits among enterprises and between the central and local governments and enterprises. The resistance is very strong. From the perspective of the interests of the whole country, it should be realized that this is an irresistible trend in adjusting the national economy and reforming the economic management system. Of course, central and local fiscal departments, as well as business departments in charge, must consider the interests of all regions, industries, and enterprises, and adopt necessary measures (such as changing the share of fiscal delivery to higher authorities, the share of retained profit, and raising or lowering tax rates) to minimize losses to all parties concerned. Everybody should realize that, under the present price system, the socialist economy cannot develop, and only by resolutely adjusting prices, and reforming the whole economic management system, can the socialist economy be freed from its present distorted pattern and develop in a healthy way.

Price Adjustments for Coal and Lumber

Adjustment of prices for many industrial goods affects the national economy and the people's livelihood substantially and must be undertaken with care. Foremost is adjustment of prices for industrial goods such as coal and timber. These affect production costs of most enterprises, and ultimately the livelihood of the citizenry. With the present shortage of energy sources, coal is China's most important source of energy. Prices for coal in China are about 50 percent lower than the world prices, and the coal industry as a whole manages only to cover costs or at most to earn a small profit. Close to half of the coal mines suffer losses. It is imperative that prices of coal be raised. But the steps toward increasing prices must be carefully arranged to avoid massive requests for price increases in other industries due to increase in cost. The negotiated prices for lumber are so much higher than planned prices that lumber producers are reluctant to deliver lumber to the state for unified allocation. They want to sell it on their own. If negotiated purchase and sales are forbidden, manufacturers will then have problems getting wood furniture, building materials, and packaging for export products. This problem must be carefully handled by phasing in price adjustments.

Price Adjustments for Agricultural Products

Purchase prices for agricultural products should continue to be raised as fiscal and economic conditions permit. At present, purchase prices for agricultural products are still relatively low. Labor compensation for peasants is still markedly below that for workers. From the long-run point of view, purchase prices for food grain must continue to be raised, while gradually reducing and finally eliminating rewards for sales over the quota.

Price Adjustments for Grain and Food

The most difficult adjustment relates to the selling prices for food grain, edible oil, cotton, and various subsidiary foodstuffs, because they greatly affect people's livelihood. In the last few years, when the governmental purchase prices for food grain and edible oil were raised, their selling prices were not changed. The excess of buying prices over selling prices was subsidized by the government budget. Losses also were substantial in the purchase of many subsidiary foodstuffs, including pork, eggs, and vegetables. According to an estimate by the General Price Bureau, these price subsidies for agricultural products reached 10 billion yuan, representing more than 10 percent of the government budget. The more that the agricultural products of these kinds are purchased, the greater will be the budget subsidies. As a result, the better the agricultural harvest, the more pressure is put on the budget. This phenomenon is abnormal. In some areas, the enthusiasm of commerce departments to buy these agricultural products has been affected. There are also serious conflicts arising from regional allocations that must depend on budget subsidies for their resolution.

In the future, a suitable time must be chosen to change these unreasonable conditions by raising the selling prices of food grain and edible oil, at least to the levels of their buying prices. At the same time, the selling prices of cotton must be raised, and suitable adjustment to the prices for cotton fabrics and blend fabrics must be made. Losses on pork, eggs, and vegetables should be gradually reduced or even eliminated by improving operation methods. While raising prices for these products, the state must correspondingly raise wages by an amount equal to the current subsidies of 10 billion yuan. The difficulty of doing this lies in the fact that the effects of price increases vary according to family size. If the state increases wages by an amount equal to the price increases, about one-third of the managerial staff and workers will benefit, one-third will suffer, and one-third will not be affected one way or another. The one-third of staff and workers who suffer are those with a large number of dependents, and the state has a responsibility to take care of them. To reduce the percentage of suffering staff and workers to below 10 percent, the state must raise wages by more than the price increase. However, these increases will not only increase budget expenditures, but also increase production costs for industries. If it is not handled well, it may even affect stability. Therefore, the state should proceed with extreme caution, although it cannot wait forever. Price departments should not drift along in their old ways, nor should they take any hasty action. Since these are important decisions relating to the national economy and the people's livelihood, all those involved in economic work and theoretical work in the country should be mobilized to participate in discussion.

CONCLUSIONS

In the past, the Chinese economic management system overemphasized planned control and ignored market regulation. Correspondingly, the price control system also overemphasized unified planned prices and ignored the regulating effect of the law of value on prices. As a result, adjustment of planned prices did not catch up with changes in production conditions, with prices deviating more and more from values. China has now begun to make use of market regulation, that is, regulation by means of the law of value. When the law of value is violated, market regulation cannot help realize the state plan and ensure balance in market supply and demand. On the contrary, it may even disrupt the state plan and lead to a proportional imbalance in the national economy. Recently, China began to make use of some market regulation and realized to its dismay that deviation of prices from values conflicts everywhere with adjustment of the national economy and reform of the economic management system. Without changing the irrational conditions created by the current price system, freely expanding the scope of market regulation is not easy. Furthermore, China must adopt various administrative measures to counteract the effects of the operation of the law of value. By doing so, the economy will not be managed solely by economic means. As adjustment of the national economy is far from being completed at present, some disturbances will result from increases in the buying prices for agricultural products and selling prices for some products. To stabilize market prices, China should not aggressively pursue adjustment of prices and reform of the price control system.

Experience in the past 30 years shows that it is very difficult to solve completely the problem of adjusting prices simply through state plans. The recent attempt to reform the economic management system indicates that current planned prices have become obstacles to various reforms. China should not limit itself to profit retention alone in its efforts to expand the autonomy of enterprises. Rather, enterprises should have the autonomy to adjust prices when conditions are favorable. Enterprises should have the power to raise prices for scarce products, reduce prices for abundant products, and reduce prices to get rid of overstocked material resources. Unified control should be exercised over major livelihood means, such as food grain, cotton fabrics, and so forth. But it may not be feasible to set a standard price for textile products, which come in many varieties and colors. It is not possible to control the price of every variety. The same applies to machine products and steel products with their many varieties and specifications. To overcome this problem, the state can set up various specialized companies in the future and allow them to set prices for different varieties and specifications under the guidance of price control departments. Coordination prices can be negotiated among companies. Buying and selling prices for many small commodities can be negotiated between producers and sellers. Price departments should comprehensively study price changes in the whole country, formulate an overall plan to adjust prices, and organize relevant departments to regulate jointly. They can also announce standard prices and magnitudes of fluctuations for important products according to market conditions to serve as references for relevant regions, departments, and enterprises in their attempts to adjust prices. Price departments should be gradually transformed from agencies that set concrete prices to ones that determine the direction and policies of price adjustment and that supervise and guide prices.

The state can consider increasing the power and responsibility over price control of provincial governments. There can be some price differentials among regions. Any disputes arising from this arrangement should be settled by the National General Price Bureau. Seasonal products can have seasonal price differentials. The size of these differentials should reflect supply and demand conditions. Prices for new products can be set independently during the trial marketing period. These products can be sold independently or through commerce departments. To encourage replacement of old products by new products, the price can be set a little bit higher on new products, and the old ones can be set comparatively lower. The commodities that are stocked in warehouses for more than one year should be sold at a discount. In a capitalist society, the prices for some commodities vary from time to time in a given period. Of course, the prices in China must be kept relatively stable. But they cannot remain unchanged either, or great losses will result because overstocked material resources cannot be handled in time. In short, the price policy in China must be both stable and flexible. After the system of unified revenues and unified expenditures and the system of unified purchase and guaranteed marketing are changed, and enterprises gain their necessary decision-making power, people will see to it that prices will not be reduced at will. At the same time, with competition among enterprises, prices will hardly be raised at will either.

The authorities in the economic field must master the art of using prices, tax rates, and interest rates as economic levers to adjust the proportional relations of the national economy. At present, price adjustments must be combined with tax rate adjustments. For example, in the case of coal and petroleum, price adjustment alone without tax rate adjustment cannot eliminate the uneven distribution of hardship and plenitude among enterprises. In the reform of the price control system, the state should free itself from the bondage of the natural economy and admit that the present economy is still a socialist commodity economy and that it must be good at maintaining the national economy in balance with market regulation. A thorough reform of the price control system should be gradually completed under the guidance of this idea.

7

Chinese Foreign Trade

Foreign trade for China is a very important component of its economy. The basic guiding principles for foreign trade are self-reliance, independence, equality, and mutual benefit. These principles have served the People's Republic of China well from its founding—when the United States and some other Western nations imposed trade embargos against it—to the present time when China has aggressively pursued an economic open-door policy that has encouraged a wide variety of measures for stimulating foreign trade.

This chapter is divided into three major sections. The first presents China's development of its foreign trade. The discussion is divided into pre- and post-1976 eras. The second section deals with the policies undertaken to reform China's foreign trade system so that the ratio of foreign trade to industrial and agricultural output can be increased. The last section deals with specific policies that have been implemented by the Chinese government for expanding foreign trade.

DEVELOPMENT OF CHINA'S FOREIGN TRADE

The history of China's foreign trade dates back more than 2,000 years to a time when Chinese silks and satins were already world famous. The trade route started from what was then the capital of China, Chang'an (present-day Xi'an, Shaanxi Province), crossed Gansu and Xinjiang, climbed over the Pamirs, crossed Central Asia and Western Asia, and finally terminated on the eastern shores of the Mediterranean. The whole route covered a distance of more than 4,300 miles, the longest inland trade route in ancient China.

Marine trade also developed, during the Sui, Tang, Song, and Yuan dynasties (A.D. 581–1568). China entered into trade relations with present-day Kampuchea, Burma, Japan, India, Sri Lanka, Nepal, Indonesia, and a number of other countries. A more dynamic foreign policy, adopted during the Ming Dynasty (1368–1640), helped widen China's trading area to include Southeast Asia, the Indian Peninsula, and the east coast of Africa. Zheng He made seven voyages to these areas and traded Chinese-made porcelains, silk fabrics, bronze and iron wares, and silver and gold for local products. Later, China's trade even extended to Latin American countries. But during the Qing Dynasty (1644–1911), foreign trade was hampered by a closed-door policy.

The Opium War of 1840 set the stage for China's gradual transformation into a semifeudal and semicolonial country, with the consequent loss of independent control over foreign trade. In the wake of a series of unequal treaties, imperialist powers secured control of China's ports, encroached upon the independence of its customs, and manipulated the operation of foreign trade institutions and facilties, namely, banking corporations, commodity inspection, insurance, shipping, piers, and warehouses. In effect, the foreign powers monopolized the foreign trade of China.

With the founding of the People's Republic, China's foreign trade entered a new stage of development. The People's Government abolished all the privileges held by the imperialists, regained control over the custom house, eliminated the semicolonial character of foreign trade, and took over the import-export businesses of the bureaucrat-capitalists. The government also established state-run foreign trade departments, adopted a policy of "utilizing, restricting, and transforming" the import-export enterprises owned by private capitalists, and announced that the state would exercise exclusive control over foreign trade—it would formulate a unified system of general and specific policies to govern foreign trade and gear it to national economic planning. This initiated an independent socialist foreign trade system.

Basic Policies of China's Foreign Trade

With the founding of the People's Republic, the government announced that "the People's Republic of China may restore and develop commercial relations with foreign governments and peoples on a basis of equality and mutual benefit." With a population of 1 billion, China must rely mainly on its own strength in building socialism. It has to rely on the labor and resourcefulness of its people and make optimum use of the country's natural resources and economic potentials. This self-reliance, however, should not be interpreted as autarchy or a closed-door policy.

As a general policy, China trades and conducts economic exchanges with other countries on the basis of self-reliance and in conformity with the principles of equality and mutual benefit and of "each supplying what the other needs." As production increases, China will actively try to expand its export trade. To expedite national economic development, it will also import various supplies, advanced technology, and key equipment. In so doing, however, it will keep within the range of its capacity to pay for the imports.

The foreign trade of China has grown faster than its national economy. There have, however, been two major setbacks. The first occurred in the late 1950s and early 1960s, when ultraleft errors, coupled with natural calamities from 1959 to 1961, precipitated a drop in production. This resulted in a decline in import-export volume between 1960 and 1962. The second setback was encountered during the "Cultural Revolution," when both industrial and agricultural production declined sharply and transportation was clogged in many places, again causing a drop in foreign trade volume in some years. However, over the past 35 years the general trend in China's foreign trade has been one of great prog-

ress. As stated above, there was a drop in foreign trade during
the Cultural Revolution. After 1976 trade started picking up rapidly again because of the recovery of the national economy, the
increase in agricultural and industrial production, and the implementation of an open-door economic policy. The average annual
growth rate for the post-1976 period has been in excess of 20 percent anually.

In general, China has been able to keep imports and exports in
reasonable balance during the past 35 years. Its planned import-
export trade has helped support domestic industrial and agricultural production and has accumulated funds for national development.

China's Foreign Trade, 1950–76

The Temporary Regulations for the Control of Foreign Trade
were approved by the Central People's Government in December
1950. This act was designed to bring export/import under the
government's control. Approximately 4,600 private foreign trade
companies employed over 35,000 personnel and accounted for about
one-third of China's total foreign trade. In the early 1950s the
socialist sector of foreign trade grew rapidly, such that by early
1956 over 99 percent of all foreign trade was accounted for by
state-run enterprises. Private foreign trade firms came under state
control in 1956, thus completing the socialist transformation.

The number of countries trading with China grew from about
40 in 1950 to over 160 by 1976. Trading volume increased from 4
billion yuan to 24 billion yuan by 1976.

China's Foreign Trade, Post-1976

Starting in 1977, China pursued an open-door economic policy
by encouraging foreign trade and developing economic cooperation programs with other countries. The basis of foreign trade has
been self-reliance, equality, and mutual benefit.

After 1976 China entered a period of rapid foreign trade expansion. As Table 7.1 shows, total foreign trade for 1983 reached a
volume of 86.01 billion yuan. China has been suffering from a
trading deficit in recent years. Generally though, China has been

able to cover these deficits through tourism revenues, remittances from Chinese residing overseas, and foreign credits.

Table 7.1
China's Total Volume of Foreign Trade (in billions of yuans)

Year	Exports	Imports	Total
1950	2.14	2.02	4.16
1952	3.75	2.71	6.46
1957	5.00	5.45	10.45
1978	18.78	16.77	35.51
1979	24.29	21.17	45.46
1982	33.64	42.00	75.64
1983	43.83	42.18	86.01

Source: Qi Wen, *China: A General Survey* (Beijing: Foreign Languages Press, 1984), p. 133.

Composition of Commodities in Foreign Trade

The composition of the commodities in foreign trade has undergone dramatic changes. In the pre-1950 era, trade consisted primarily of imports of consumer goods and exports of agricultural as well as handicraft products. Since the founding of the People's Republic, imports of the means of production or producer goods have been increasing faster than other import goods. Apart from agricultural and handicraft products, exports of manufactured goods have expanded, particularly textile and light industry products. China began to export petroleum in 1973, and simultaneously it also exported heavy industrial products. Compared with 1953, the relative shares in the composition of exports for 1979 were as follows: agricultural and handicraft products fell from 55.7 to 23.1 percent; textile and light industrial products rose from 26.9 to 45 percent; heavy industrial products rose from 17.1 to 31.9 percent.

China's post-1950 imports were generally capital goods. Between 1952 and 1976, China imported complete plants for building machinery, motor vehicles, electronics, and so forth, along with capital goods imports in communications, coal mining, metal refining, and power generation. These imports built China's industrial base.

China also increased its import of consumer goods to meet the material and cultural needs of the populace. Import changes from 1953 to 1979 were as follows: capital goods declined from 90 to 80 percent; consumer goods increased from 10 to 20 percent. It is expected that this trend in increased imports of consumer goods will continue.

Despite the rapid growth of China's foreign trade, the total value is still comparatively low, not only lower than that of the industrial countries, but also than that of some developing countries. The total value of China's exports accounts for less than 1 percent of the world exports. The total value of commodities the state procured for export accounts for about 5 percent of the country's total industrial and agricultural output value, a ratio far below that of other countries. It is obvious that this situation is not compatible with the requirements of socialist modernization, nor with the development of China's foreign relations. Energetic measures are now being taken by the government to promote further growth of the country's foreign trade.

Trade Relations with Foreign Countries

With the imposition of a trade embargo by the U.S. and a number of other countries against China in October 1950, China was forced to choose the Soviet Union and other socialist countries for trading partners. In subsequent years, trade with some Western European countries expanded, partially in response to the 1954 Geneva agreement. By the mid-1950s about 78 percent of China's foreign trade was with the Soviet Union and its allies as opposed to only 22 percent with Western Europe and other countries.

The Soviet Union in 1960 decided to withdraw its technical personnel from China. This action resulted in bringing to a halt a large number of projects financed and/or technically supported by the Soviets. Chinese plans for economic and industrial development were seriously affected. With decline in Chinese-Soviet trade, China started to place increased emphasis on trade with the West. Japan exported two vinylon plants in 1962. Additional engineering, petroleum, mining, and other equipment were imported from Japan and Western countries.

The flow of imports and technology was interrupted in the late 1960s due to the Cultural Revolution. Importation of new technology and equipment was resumed in 1972, although now the emphasis was on importing complete plants.

In recent years, the volume of trade between China and other developing countries has shown continuous growth. In line with the policy of supplying each other's needs and doing so within each other's capacity, China has exported to other developing countries mainly industrial goods, such as tools, machine tools, hardware for construction, complete sets of equipment, and light industrial and textile goods. China's imports from these countries consist mainly of agricultural and animal husbandry products and mineral and chemical products. In recent years China has signed trade agreements or protocols with many countries in Asia and Africa.

Among the developed countries, Japan is China's largest trading partner. Geographical and economic factors have created favorable conditions for the development of Sino-Japanese trade. In 1972 China and Japan established diplomatic relations. The signing of the China-Japan Long-Trade Agreement in 1978 served as a strong stimulus for trade between these two countries. Japan now accounts for about 25 percent of China's total foreign trade. Japan's major exports to China have been machinery and other equipment, iron and steel products, and chemical fertilizers. China's main exports to Japan have been agricultural products and crude oil.

Western Europe is China's second largest trading partner. The signing of a long-term trade agreement in 1978 between the European Economic Community (EEC) and China and EEC's granting of preferential treatment to China in 1980 have helped stimulate trade. Trading with Western Europe now accounts for about 15 percent of China's trading volume.

China-U.S. trade resumed in 1972, after a hiatus of 20 years, with the signing of the Shanghai Communiqué. The establishment of diplomatic relations in January 1979, Deng Xiaoping's visit to the United States, the formation of the Sino-U.S. Joint Economic Committee in March 1979, and the signing of a bilateral trade agreement in July 1979 further stimulated trade. In February 1980 the Agreement on Trade Relations came into effect, and each nation gave the other most-favored nation status. The United States now accounts for about 8 percent of China's foreign trade. From time to time, China has expressed its concern about import restrictions on items such as textiles and garments and about export restrictions on high-technology items. Removal or relaxation of some of these restrictions could result in increased growth for China-U.S. trade.

The Soviet Union, Poland, East Germany, Bulgaria, Czechoslovakia, and Hungary account for less than 2 percent of China's foreign trade. However, recently there are some indications pointing to increased levels of trade between China and these countries. Trading with Romania, Yugoslavia, and Korea has grown steadily.

Hong Kong and Macao occupy positions of significance in China's foreign trade. Hong Kong is not only China's largest source of foreign currencies but also serves as the largest transit port for China's exports. Many of the goods exported to Macao and Hong Kong are, of course, designated for resale in other countries. Hong Kong presently accounts for over one-third of China's total foreign currency earnings.

As the area of trade widens, reciprocal visits and friendly contacts between the governments of China and other countries, and between Chinese and foreign trade circles, are on the increase. By the end of 1985, China had participated in about 400 international trade fairs and trade exhibitions outside China and had helped business persons from more than 25 countries put up over 180 industrial, technological, and trade exhibitions in China.

Furthermore, since 1957 China has set up periodic export commodities fairs in order to hold trade talks with foreign business persons. The Chinese Export Commodities Fair has been held in Guangzhou every spring and autumn.

Import of Technology and Complete Sets of Equipment

In the 1950s China imported advanced technology and complete sets of equipment mostly from the Soviet Union. In accord with the agreements signed between China and the Soviet Union during its First Five-Year Plan (1953–57), imports consisted of 156 trade items involving metallurgy, automobiles, machinery, telecommunications, and so on. This trade was important for setting up an initial base for China's later industrial development. In the early 1960s the Soviet Union reneged on the bilateral contracts signed between the two countries. This caused China tremendous difficulties for its economic development program. Due to the sharp drop in Sino-Soviet trade, China bought technology from Japan and Western Europe. From 1962 to 1966, China's imports of technology and equipment from Japan and Western Europe amounted to 84 trade items including petroleum, chemicals, matallurgy, electronics, precision instruments, and so forth. The import of technology came to a standstill during the Cultural Revolution and was not resumed until 1972. From 1972 to 1977, China signed a number of contracts with industrial corporations in Japan, France, West Germany, the United States, Italy, and Britain that were valued at more than $4 billion in U.S. dollars. These imports were used mainly for the development of the petrochemical, chemical fertilizer, coal, iron, and steel industries.

After the Cultural Revolution, a decision was made to speed up the four modernizations, and more technology and urgently needed equipments were imported. But import volume was overextended in 1978. The value of contracts entered into that year amounted to 18.78 billion yuan. This became a heavy burden on the national economy. Hereafter, the import of technology will be geared to national economic needs, particularly to meeting the light industry and textile industry and other weak links in the economy. Also, special attention will be paid to integrating the import of technology with the updating of existing enterprises.

REFORM OF CHINA'S FOREIGN TRADE SYSTEM

It has been typical of China's past that economic policies, including those related to foreign trade, have been highly centralized. Given that a number of Western countries, including the United States, had imposed a trade embargo on China, centralized decisions with regard to foreign trade made sense. In the early

1950s, China's main trading partners were countries with centrally planned economies. Foreign trade typically occurred under bilateral trade agreements that specified goods to be traded and prices to paid. However, with the souring of relations with the Soviet Union and with a shift from a closed-door to an open-door economic policy, the problems associated with a centrally planned foreign trade system have become more apparent.

A number of problems can be identified with China's foreign trade system. First, concentration of power and administrative control diminished the enthusiasm of various regions and departments to pursue exports aggressively. Second, since manufacturers were not part of the sales negotiations, there usually was a disparity between production and marketing. Third, the quality and quantity of export items have varied. Fourth, quite often imports of certain types of capital goods have not been appropriate. Fifth, imports often cannot be justified on an economic basis. Thus, there has been an emphasis in recent years on reforming the foreign trade system.

Over the past few years, a number of reforms have been initiated in the foreign trade system. Guangdong and Fujian provinces, the municipalities of Beijing, Shanghai, and Tianjin and other coastal provinces, and cities have begun trading with foreign countries directly. More and more commodities are being gradually turned over to local foreign trade departments, which are now allowed to engage in compensation trade and in processing semi-finished products. Approved by state agencies, some departments have established joint production and joint ventures with foreign enterprises for imports and exports. Although the reforms have promoted foreign trade, they have also created some problems, mostly in management. These problems have been frequently mentioned by China's trading partners. Transient chaos is practically inevitable in the process of reform, but the overall development is sound, and the chaos will soon be over. China can eventually overcome the problems when the Chinese foreign trade system becomes more streamlined. The overriding idea behind the reform is to motivate all provinces and municipalities and all departments and enterprises to become involved in foreign trade, and to delegate to them more power to make decisions to achieve better coordination between production and distribution and to speed up the rate of economic development.

Now that China has entered a new stage of development with modernization as its central task, foreign trade needs to grow faster than ever before. Some reforms have been introduced in recent years in the foreign trade structure. The guiding principles for these reforms have been to overcome overcentralization of management, rigid control, and dislocation between production and marketing, to bring the initiative of all quarters into full play and to expand foreign trade. Meanwhile, it is necessary to emphasize a proper degree of unified leadership in order to maintain unity in the policy, planning, and stance in foreign trade. Under this unified guidance, management and business accounting are conducted at different levels, and each level is responsible for its own profits and losses. A variety of measures, as explained below, have been taken to reform the foreign trade structure.

The national import and export corporations have decentralized their authority, turning over much of it to the provinces and municipalities. Except for a few goods, the export business of all the products produced locally in Guangdong and Fujian provinces is now being handled entirely by provincial corporations. Foreign trade corporations that have been set up in Beijing, Tianjin, and Shanghai are vested with the power for conducting foreign trade. Other provinces have expanded their foreign trade operations and can conduct direct transactions with foreign firms. The municipalities and the enterprises share the foreign income earned, thus providing the latter with strong incentives to export. A number of municipalities have formed special divisions or enterprises to encourage foreign trade. Examples include the Beijing Economic Construction Corporation and the Fujian Investment Company.

Some of the export goods that were previously handled by corporations under the Ministry of Foreign Trade are now being handled by import and export corporations newly established by the departments in charge of production. This has also opened new foreign trade channels, the first one being the China Machinery Import and Export Corporation. Subsequent corporations have been established in electronics, aviation, metallurgy, motion pictures, and so on.

Different forms of association of industries and foreign trade enterprises are being tried, and experimental foreign trade enterprises, based on associations of enterprises, are being developed.

While continuing to undertake and fulfill state plans for foreign trade, the import-export corporations under the Ministry of Foreign Trade are expanding their commission business and organizing joint import and export operations. Wherever feasible, the producer enterprises are permitted to take part in international trade activities and negotiations with foreign firms. Thus, the producers are establishing direct contacts with buyers, and production is being geared to market demand.

A system has been implemented for allowing localities to retain part of their foreign exchange earnings so they can import necessary supplies. Preferential customs duties are provided for material imported for the purpose of expanding exports.

Some coastal areas in Guangdong and Fujian provinces have been set aside as special economic zones where more flexible administrative policies than those applied in other parts of the country are being tried.

Structural reforms in foreign trade are being undertaken in different provinces in the light of their specific conditions. The general orientation of these structural reforms is to change the foreign trade departments from agencies doing foreign trade with purchased goods into enterprises doing foreign trade by acting as sales agents and rendering services, and to base foreign trade on conglomerates of enterprises. This cannot be achieved overnight but has been set as a goal to be reached step by step.

POLICIES FOR EXPANDING CHINA'S FOREIGN TRADE

China has taken strong measures to develop foreign trade and expand economic cooperations with foreign countries. It has also adopted appropriate methods for raising funds from external sources that are in keeping with international practice. China's experience during the last 35 years has demonstrated that the key to expanded foreign trade exists in boosting exports. Whenever exports have risen rapidly, Chinese foreign trade has also expanded, because exports have provided the means for importing more. Exports have determined imports. Only by expanding exports can China earn foreign exchange to pay for imports of advanced technology and equipment. Consequently, the principle governing China's foreign trade can be briefly stated as "exports take precedence, but exports and imports are interrelated." China will import what it can pay for by exports, and it will seek to balance imports against exports. Ideally, the trade balance here should be construed as global balance and not just as balance with an individual country in every year.

To promote exports, China has tried to pay attention to those commodities that are to be exported. For years, the problem facing China in export has been that few of its products could meet international standards of quality, style, and packaging. It lacks the means of transportation and communication facilities. To cope with these problems, the government, in recent years, has adopted a series of measures to promote trade and has created conditions more favorable for trade expansion.

Increasing Quality and Production of Export Commodities

China's exports, while increasing, are a relatively minor portion of its industrial and agricultural output. China is placing increased emphasis on quality, appearance, durability, style, and packaging as means for expanding its exports. To some extent, exporters are receiving priority in the distribution of raw materials, power, and transportation. This increased emphasis on exports causes a dilemma for China's planners—basically, how to trade off the benefits of increased domestic consumption versus the benefits of foreign currencies earned by exporting. It is an issue that may find its own resolution as China reaches the economic "takeoff" stage.

Flexible Methods of Trade

A variety of flexible methods of trade that had been abandoned during the Cultural Revolution are being emphasized again. China has begun to develop effectively its brand names for selected products with the intention of establishing brand loyalty. It has also emphasized private label manufacturing, that is, manufacturing products under a label designated by the buyer. Similarly, China's exporters have not hesitated to utilize neutral labeling, the process in which Chinese trademarks or country of origin are not displayed. In addition, Chinese firms are manufacturing goods in conformance with the design and packaging specifications of buyers. These strategies are resulting in expanded exports.

Recognizing that it has a vast pool of workers whose wages are highly competitive, China has emphasized processing and assembly work. Chinese firms, which receive processing or assembly fees based on contractual provisions, are provided with raw or partially processed products, and deliver finished goods to their clients. Currently, China has about 10,000 processing or assembly contracts, with the vast majority of them concentrated in the Guangdong province. Other areas for processing and assembly include Shanghai, Fujian, Jiangsu, Guangxi, and Beijing. The typical products are textiles, garments, tools, machinery, and electronics.

Funds Borrowed from Foreign Governments

China benefits from export credits provided by foreign governments or banks to facilitate trade with China. The French government, for example, may extend export credit so that a French firm can export machinery to China. This export credit, or loan, is then repaid in installments.

A number of governments have provided loans to China. For example, the Japanese Overseas Cooperation Funds have provided China with loans to finance six construction projects. These loans typically have low interest rates and extended payout periods. The Export-Import Bank of Japan has also provided funds for coal mining and oil extraction.

Additionally, China has received loans from the International Monetary Fund and the World Bank. China has been seeking long-term low interest rates from various governments and international agencies to help develop its natural resources and industrial base.

Commodity Credit

Commodity credit refers to financing measures related to compensatory trade and to processing and assembling. In commodity credit, technology, equipment, and raw or partially processed or assembled materials are provided by clients who are willing to accept commodities and products as payment. One procedure in compensatory trade is for the client to accept products manufactured by equipment and technology and materials supplied by it. A second method is "counterpurchase" in which the client agrees to purchase nonrelated products. Commodity trade received a significant boost from Regulations Governing the Promotion of Processing and Assembly Business and on Medium- and Small-Scale Compensation Trade Involving Foreign Firms, which was adopted in September 1979.

The People's Republic views compensatory trade as benefiting both China and its foreign client. China benefits from imported technology, foreign exchange earned from exporting related products, and increased utilization of its labor force. The client benefits from access to raw materials and low-cost labor.

Certain problems are associated with commodity credit. Often it is difficult to negotiate mutually beneficial contracts for buying the finished products. With counterpurchase trade, clients often insist on buying products that are highly competitive on international markets. But, from China's perspective, these are the products that would sell well internationally anyway and earn foreign currencies for it. Secondly, at times China is offered obsolete technology at high prices, something that it does not want. However, despite these obstacles, commodity trade is highly viable if approached from a viewpoint of mutual benefit and friendly cooperation.

Joint Ventures

China recognizes two types of joint ventures: contractual and equity. In a contractual joint venture, the foreign firm may provide some combination of technology, equipment, managerial know-how, and so on, while the Chinese firm provides land, building, and labor. Profits are shared on a contractual basis. In an equity joint venture, both partners contribute equity capital and share proportionally in profits and losses.

The Law of the People's Republic of China on Chinese-Foreign Joint Ventures was adopted in July 1979 and governs joint ventures in China. According to the law, foreign investments and related profits are protected by the Chinese government. Currently, about 200 joint ventures, with foreign capital well in excess of $3 billion, are in operation in China.

Economic Zones

Selected areas in the Guangdong and Fujian provinces have been designated as economic zones. Economic zones are designed to be more encompassing than either free trade zones or export-processing zones. The economic zones, besides attracting foreign investment and export-oriented industries, are also seeking to attract technology and develop tourism. The economic zones have great potential for technical centers, joint ventures, compensatory trade business, tourism, and sole foreign investments.

The economic zones provide preferential treatment to investors. Goods to be exported from these economic zones are not subject to duties. A variety of other benefits, such as reduced taxes and tax exemption on reinvested profits, also accrue to investors in economic zones.

CONCLUSIONS

From a long-range viewpoint, the industrial base that China has built so far over the years has indeed provided a material and technological foundation for further development. With the reform of the existing management system, the rates of growth should be faster and the levels of technology higher, thus enhancing exports. This situation is particularly true with regard to labor-intensive industries and traditional arts and handicrafts. China's rich resources and abundance of labor are the assets that should be tapped. Moreover, China is also rich in mineral resources. Its reserves of coal and nonferrous metals are plentiful, and efforts are being made to exploit mineral ores for export. The prospects for China's foreign trade are bright. It is estimated that in future years the rates of growth for foreign trade will be higher than for the gross national product. Therefore, the share of exports in industrial and agricultural production will gradually rise.

The composition of China's imports will not undergo any substantial changes. It is reasonable to assume that capital goods and equipment will still dominate China's imports, and so will some metals and raw materials for the chemical industry as well as food grains. Substantial changes are not expected in the composition of China's exports, with farm products and native sundries and textiles continuing to be major exports. Efforts, however, will be made to promote exports of minerals and chemicals. Although petroleum still plays an important role, it is not likely to expand rapidly in the near future. An increment in coal exports is not only possible but probable. With the readjustment of the economy, the expansion of production, and advances in technology, China will export more machinery and electric appliances than it did in previous years, just as planned.

Some government officials and business persons abroad are worried that too much export of Chinese textiles and light industrial products might flood the international markets, and they believe that if this happens it will adversely affect the exports and domestic markets of other developing countries. But such worries are groundless because China has an enormous home market where production falls short of domestic demand, particularly for textiles and light industrial products. China will not, therefore, push for export of these products without restraint. Moreover, China's policy is too carry out foreign trade according to the needs and capacities of both parties. At present, the share of China's exports of textiles and light industrial products is such that its impact on the international market is insignificant. It must be pointed out, however, that only when China exports can it import. A country may have great import potential provided that it is able to export. This fact is simple and plain.

Apart from pursuing the traditional means of international trade, China has put into effect in recent years other measures to promote foreign trade, including joint production, joint ventures, compensation trade, and the processing of semifinished products. These measures are only a start. China will continue to explore new avenues to boost its trade with other countries.

8

Regulatory Framework

Since its founding, the People's Republic of China has undergone many changes in its regulatory framework. Initially, the changes were designed in response to or in anticipation of changes in economic, political, and social changes. More recently, with China becoming more receptive to foreign enterprises, the changes have also focused on the role of foreign firms in the Chinese economy. For the foreign firm seeking to enter into a joint venture agreement in China, understanding the regulatory framework becomes important. The Chinese banking and tax systems are discussed in this chapter.

A foreign firm in China will invariably have to deal with the People's Bank of China and the Bank of China. This chapter provides a historical perspective on the banking system in China and explains the workings of the major Chinese banking institutions.

The section on the tax system discusses the major reforms that have been mentioned about the Chinese taxation system. Also discussed are the tax laws as they apply to joint ventures and foreign enterprises.

THE BANKING SYSTEM

Shortly after the founding of the People's Republic, the first order of business for the banking industry was to try to bring China's raging inflationary price spirals under control. In the decade preceding the republic's founding, the money supply and the prices had increased many billionfold. After its founding, there was little letup in the inflation rates. Continued sporadic fighting, relief for flood victims, and postwar rehabilitation activities all required large state expenditures. With the imbalance between governmental revenues and expenditures, the state kept printing more money. In the meantime, speculators hoarded gold, silver, and other commodities. At this time, the state made a concerted effort to control inflation by reducing speculation and balancing its revenues and expenditures. In March 1950 three significant decisions for reducing inflation were made: major items of revenue collection and expenditure were centralized; transfer of materials was centralized so that domestic supply and demand could be regulated; and cash at the People's Bank was centralized.

Prices stabilized shortly after these measures were implemented. Two years later, industrial and agricultural output had been increased by about 44 percent, while price had declined about 7 percent. This stability in prices also resulted in the decline of bartering and panic buying. Finally, in March 1955, the state issued new currency called Renminbi (RMB), thus signaling total control over inflation.

During the First Five-Year Plan (1953–57), banks actively provided funds for state-run enterprises, for state purchase, and for state subsidies. Generally, prices were stable during this time.

During the Great Leap Forward, there was some emphasis on abolishing money as a medium of exchange. Banks started to loan funds without fully evaluating the economic consequences. This indiscriminate extension of credit resulted not only in large losses for banks but also produced imbalances in revenues and expenditures. By 1961 the money supply had doubled, compared to 1957, resulting in rising prices and a declining standard of living.

At the beginning of the recovery period, the People's Bank was given ministerial-level status to allow it to serve its role better. Credit procedures were reimposed, and collections were emphasized. The net results were twofold. Some of the weaker enterprises, which relied heavily on credit, were forced to shut down, scale back operations, or merge with other enterprises. On the other hand, the economically viable enterprises were able to compete more effectively for funds. With the concomitant reduction in the supply of money in circulation, inflation was reduced, and reasonably stable prices prevailed in the marketplace.

The Cultural Revolution created a disastrous situation for banks, which were labeled "economic bureaucracies." Insurance was considered a method for protecting the interests of the bourgeois and thus was abolished. Interest was viewed as a device for exploiting the working class and, therefore, was reduced dramatically. The insistence by banks on loan repayments was correlated to demand by landlords for payments, and so rules for loan repayments were abolished. All of these actions resulted in increases in the amount of money in circulation, decline in national output, and the stockpiling of obsolete goods. With the end of the Cultural Revolution, extended reforms of the Chinese banking system were necessary.

Reforms of the Banking System

The government has emphasized economic improvement in recent years. Three reforms undertaken in 1979 are especially important: enterprises were allowed more decision-making flexibility; emphasis was placed on market-based regulation; and banks were allowed to make short- and medium-term equipment loans. The last reform was important because, while enterprises could retain some profits and receive some depreciation funds, they did not have enough money for expanding production. By providing short- and medium-term credit, banks were able to fund acquisition of new technology, product innovation, and expanded production.

The People's Bank of China established a short- and medium-term loan ceiling of 5 billion yuan in 1980. These funds were utilized for four purposes: (1) supporting expanded production in the durable consumer goods and textile industries; (2) supporting the retooling efforts of obsolete factories; (3) increasing measures to conserve energy; and (4) developing tourism and transportation.

124

Mathur and Chen

The loans have been particularly effective in increasing output, employment, profits, and taxes paid.

The Agricultural Bank of China and the People's Construction Bank of China have also provided short- and medium-term loans successfully. In fact, the success of this reform indicates that eventually all enterprises, with the exception of those in areas such as agriculture, tourism, commerce, education, and health services, will see their financial appropriations replaced by repayable loans from banks.

Some of the other reforms carried out by banks include: partially utilizing the profit-sharing concept in selected bank branches; decentralizing bank administration; viewing branch offices as profit centers; decentralizing deposit and credit management; reinstituting domestic insurance; offering loans based on needs rather than on state plans; adjusting interest paid on deposits; charging higher rates for delinquent accounts; instituting market research related to bank functions; and gathering information on foreign markets and banking trends.

Anticipated Future Reforms

While the banks have made substantial reforms to date, there is room for still further reforms. Banks, for example, would be interested in total autonomy in providing loans to enterprises. This implies that the government would establish credit policies and lending policies. However, the banks would be free to engage in loan application evaluations and would determine the merit of the loan, the amount of funds needed, and the repayment structure for the loan. Along with the responsibility for administering loans, banks would also be responsible for managing their nonperforming (delinquent) loans.

Banks would also prefer to regulate interest rates charged on loans. Overall interest rate levels would be periodically adjusted by the People's Bank, and the other banks would adjust their rates accordingly.

Finally, banks would prefer to have total administrative control over their operations. Banks would be free to expand or reduce their operations, add or delete offices, adjust the size of the staff, and engage in profit sharing.

While the banking industry is very much interested in additional reforms, it is anticipated that reforms will not come very rapidly, partially due to a shortage of technically qualified employees. The number of colleges, institutes, and universities offering programs in the banking area is limited, resulting in a critical shortage of qualified personnel. Some banks are moving toward starting, or have already started, their own training schools, and it is expected that the level of trained banking personnel will increase at an adequate rate.

MAJOR BANKS

The People's Bank of China, the Bank of China, the Agricultural Bank of China, and the People's Construction Bank of China are major banks in the republic.

The People's Bank of China

The People's Bank of China has ministerial-level status in the government and acts as the state bank (equivalent to the Federal Reserve System in the United States). Its major responsibilities include: issuing RMB; implementing governmental policies related to banking and interest rates; providing treasury functions for the government and managing its revenues and disbursements; regulating the monetary market; regulating gold and silver transactions; providing loans to enterprises; and encouraging savings by individuals.

The bank has 29 provincial branches and more than 15,000 branches and sub-branches in counties, towns, municipalities, and industrial and mining areas. About 350,000 people are employed at the People's Bank.

The Bank of China

The Bank of China deals exclusively with foreign exchange. Its major functions include: handling foreign currency deposits; handling RMB deposits related to foreign exchange; handling export-import credit; setting foreign currency accounts related to joint ventures, compensatory trades, and so on, as well as buying and selling foreign currencies; handling foreign currency payments and receipts; managing foreign exchange reserves; and supporting increased levels of exports.

The bank has about 120 domestic branches in cities, ports, and areas where foreign exchange business is transacted. Its overseas branches are located in London, New York, Tokyo, Hong Kong, Singapore, and Luxembourg. Additionally, it has correspondent relations with banks in numerous countries.

The Agricultural Bank of China

The Agricultural Bank of China, as its name implies, is involved with banking policies and procedures in the rural areas. Its services include deposits from agricultural enterprises and collectives; support services for rural enterprises and collectives; distribution of agricultural appropriations; operations of the rural credit cooperatives; rural credit plans; coordination and control of agricultural aid; and assistance in modernizing agriculture.

The bank has about 30,000 branches and sub-branches with a total of 300,000 employees.

One of the activities of the bank is to oversee the rural credit cooperatives. These cooperatives are collectively owned and are fully responsible for their profits and losses. These cooperatives provide rural banking services and help with the modernization of agriculture. A cooperative is established wherever there is a commune or collective. If a bank is present also, then the cooperative associates with the bank. There are approximately 60,000 credit cooperatives in existence.

The People's Construction Bank of China

The People Construction Bank of China is responsible for the management of construction funds. Its major responsibilities are to provide construction loans to a wide variety of enterprises that have the ability to repay loans; provide construction funds for enterprises and units that do not have the ability to repay loans, for example, health, educational, and administrative units; and provide loans for joint ventures and firms involved with compensatory trade. The bank has about 2,600 offices.

THE TAX SYSTEM

Taxes serve a variety of purposes, including financing the activities of the government and implementing social goals. In a socialist country, such as China, the public sector of the economy dominates, and, therefore, the government should be able to finance its activities and implement social goals without imposing taxes. The government could easily carry out these activities because it obtains the profits of state-run enterprises and because it has the ability to adjust upward or downward payments that transfer resources between various sectors of the economy.

Why then does China have a tax system? Several reasons can be advanced for China's utilization of a national tax system. First, the revenue generation and income consumption needs of the various sectors of the economy are not fully balanced. One sector may generate income beyond its consumption needs, while a second may need additional income. Taxes provide one means for transferring income or wealth from the first sector to the second. Another reason is that, in the absence of taxes, cyclic fluctuations in incomes in different economic sectors can lead to over- and underconsumption. Taxation and subsidies help smooth out the effect of these fluctuations. Third, the government can raise funds from the nonpublic enterprises only through taxation. For these major reasons, it is deemed appropriate for China to have a tax system.

Background of the Tax System

When the People's Republic was founded, taxes were imposed to support the revolutionary war and to provide finances for the development of a war-affected economy. Fourteen different categories of taxes were implemented, including income, property, customs, excise, and inheritance taxes. Prior to, and during the First Five-Year Plan, the tax structure was simplified, resulting in the elimination of taxes on wages and inheritances.

Another tax reform was undertaken in 1958, this time resulting in the simplification of the tax categories. Tax rates were also readjusted, and additional tax reforms have been undertaken periodically. There are two salient characteristics of the current tax system. First, the main burden of taxes falls on production and distribution. These two sectors of the economy provide about 75 percent of all taxes raised by the government. Second, individual taxes have been deemphasized, the main reasons being that there is not much variation in income levels and that wage levels have tended to be on the low side.

Some Considerations in Reforming the Tax System

A variety of reforms have been proposed or discussed for re-forming the tax system. First, with China opening its doors to foreign investments and with its emphasis on industrial moderni-zation, the economic sectors have become more diversified. In-comes generated by joint ventures and by public and collective ownerships are the result of different government policies and, as such, should be subject to different taxation standards.

Two enterprises producing identical products may have differ-ent levels of profitability. Part of this difference may be explained by differences in worker productivity and/or managerial skills ex-isting in the enterprise. But some of this difference may also be accounted for by factors beyond the control of the enterprise—factors such as access to raw materials, age of the production equipment, level of technology being utilized, and so on. In the past, this income differential was not of major concern, since in-come was turned over to the government anyway. But now, with increased emphasis on decentralized decision making, profit reten-tion, and a market orientation, these differential incomes due to technology and equipment are a cause for concern. It seems rea-sonable that a revised tax system would take into consideration factors producing these income differentials and allow for adjust-ments that emphasize worker productivity and managerial skills.

Currently, inter-enterprise trade is affected by the repeated tax-ation of semifinished and industrial products. This had encour-aged enterprises to expand vertically so that their dependence on semifinished and industrial products is minimized. While this re-sults in self-sufficiency for the enterprises involved, it also keeps them from specializing and thus increasing their productivity. A value-added tax would alleviate this problem by taxing only the incremental value of semifinished and industrial products as they move from enterprise to enterprise. Prime candidates for the value-added tax are the industrial and farm machinery industries.

Foreign firms establishing joint ventures in China often provide funds through loans. Other times, joint ventures are financed through equity capital that requires periodic dividend payments. Additionally, foreign firms may insist on receiving royalties on patent licenses, and they may charge management fees. Thus, China's expanding relationships with foreign firms have resulted in dividends on foreign capital, interest on foreign loans, royalties on patent licenses, and management fees. These payments to foreign firms and individuals impinge on China's rights to safeguard its economic interests and maintain its sovereignty. A reasonable tax system should allow for adequate taxation of dividends, interest, royalties, and fees for maintaining equality.

China tries to regulate demand and supply as well as production and consumption through pricing. Occasionally, this will result in losses for some enterprises and excess profits for others. Judicious use of taxes would adjust for these profits and losses not related to worker productivity and managerial skills.

TAXATION OF INDIVIDUAL INCOMES

China imposed a wage tax for individuals in 1950, but the taxes were never levied because wages had been relatively low. Now, with more Chinese earning wages abroad and with more foreigners earning income in China, the tax law for individuals is being enforced. The tax law has the following characteristics: (1) taxes are to be paid on all foreign and domestic income by persons residing in China for a period greater than one year; (2) taxes are to be paid only on the Chinese portion of earnings by persons not residing in China or those residing in China for less than one year.

Wages, compensation for personal services, royalties, dividends, rental property income, and other incomes are subject to taxes. A variety of income categories such as prizes and awards for achievements, interest income from domestic financial institutions, welfare benefits, retirement benefits, salaries paid to diplomats, and earnings designated as tax free by the Ministry of Finance are not subject to taxes.

Individual earnings are subject to both progressive and proportional taxes. Wages up to a maximum of 800 yuan per month are exempt from taxes. Wages in excess of 800 yuan per month are subject to progressive tax rates that range from 5 to 45 percent. Income from other sources, such as personal services, royalties, dividends, rental property, and so on, is subject to a flat tax rate of 20 percent. Taxable income related to personal services, royalties, and rental properties allows for an adjustment for expenses.

TAXATION OF JOINT AND FOREIGN VENTURES

The tax system for joint ventures differs from the one that applies to foreign enterprises operating in China.

Taxation of Joint Ventures

In 1979 China formulated a comprehensive joint venture law that established guidelines for foreign firms that are interested in operating ventures jointly with Chinese firms. The basic principle behind this law is equality and mutual benefit. In 1980 the Third Plenary Session of the Fifth National People's Congress adopted the Income Tax Law of the People's Republic of China Concerning Joint Ventures with Chinese and Foreign Investment.

The law applies to joint ventures based in the People's Republic between Chinese and foreign firms. Income from operations in China as well as from branch operations outside of China is subject to the tax law. Taxes are imposed on all sources of income irrespective of whether they are derived from operations, or sources such as management and licensing fees received, and interest and dividend income. The tax rate is a flat 33 percent.

The 33 percent tax rate applies to the manufacturing, assembling, and service industries. The tax situation for joint ventures in the extractive industries is different and more complex. Firms planning on joint ventures in petroleum, mining, natural gas, and drilling are subject to these laws.

The tax law has a variety of preferential treatments for joint ventures under certain circumstances. First, for joint ventures that are expected to operate for a minimum of ten years, first-year income is totally free from taxes, and second- and third-year incomes are provided a 50 percent reduction in taxes. Second, joint ventures in low profit areas, such as agriculture, and in remote areas are allowed a 15 to 30 percent reduction in income taxes for another ten years following the first three years, which, of course, receive the tax benefits mentioned above. The first-year income refers to the first year in which income is earned, not the first year of operations.

One way in which China encourages additional foreign investment is to provide an incentive for reinvesting earnings. A foreign joint venture partner that reinvests its share of the profits for at least five years receives a refund of 40 percent of taxes paid on the profits reinvested.

The tax law also allows for depreciation and losses. Under certain circumstances, the joint venture can use accelerated depreciation procedures in calculating its income. Finally, operational losses can be carried forward for a maximum of five years and can be charged off against future operating incomes.

Taxation of Foreign Enterprises

The Income Tax Law of the People's Republic of China Concerning Foreign Enterprises was implemented in 1981. Foreign enterprises are defined to be foreign firms that are conducting business operations in China, either independently, or cooperatively with Chinese enterprises. Also covered are foreign firms that do not have business operations in China but receive dividends, interest income, royalties, management fees, and rental and other income from Chinese sources. Foreign enterprises are subject to progressive tax rates that vary from 20 to 50 percent. The law has provisions for preferential treatment and tax exemption for taxable income.

CONCLUSIONS

This chapter has provided a look at the banking and tax systems in China. By no means should it be understood that China has reached an equilibrium stage with regard to reforms in either the banking or the tax areas. The banking system would like to move toward methods of operation that are more familiar to Western business persons. However, the anticipated changes will be slow in coming.

The tax system as it applies to joint ventures and foreign enterprises is relatively new. The tax laws provide a general framework but not much in terms of very specific details. It is expected that both tax laws will be revised over time, through formal actions and informally through interpretations by Chinese regulations. One reasonable precaution is to have inserted in the joint venture agreement a clause that allows for modification of the agreement if the effective tax rates are raised. Additionally, it may be feasible to negotiate a tax reduction or exemption beyond the normal time limits.

9

Chinese Perspectives on Joint Ventures

The much-heralded joint venture between American Motors Corporation (AMC) and China that resulted in the formation of the Beijing Jeep Corporation in May 1984 started to turn sour after not even one year of operation. The main problem was that China was not willing to permit the joint venture to use scarce foreign exchange to buy jeep kits from Canada. The joint venture was a good symbol of China's open door policy. Its problems were even better symbols of China's emphasis on self-reliance. The joint venture would have turned out to be much more successful if AMC had looked at China's open door policy and its need for self-reliance in tandem and tried negotiating a joint venture that would have emphasized local manufacturing rather than assembly.

This chapter provides the Chinese perspective on joint ventures. The first section discusses China's open door and self-reliance policies. Subsequent sections examine employment creation, development of China's infrastructure and energy industries, transfer

This chapter is based on a working paper by the authors and Lynette L. Knowles of Ohio State University.

of technology, and agricultural and industrial modernization, which are some of China's goals in entering into joint ventures.

CHINA'S OPEN DOOR AND SELF-RELIANCE POLICIES

Ever since its founding, the People's Republic has emphasized self-reliance as the basis for Chinese society. For China, self-reliance has meant that it will rely on its own resources to achieve its social and economic gains. Self-reliance has implied independence from foreign sources in developing China's economy, improving agricultural production, establishing the path for cultural values, providing a reasonable standard of living, and so forth.

This policy of self-reliance was followed with strong rigidity during the Cultural Revolution, with anything foreign being rejected out of hand. China's exposure to foreign countries and firms, and vice versa, was seriously damaged in this time period. One of the results of this policy was that during the Cultural Revolution the Chinese economy suffered.

Subsequently, China's leaders took the approach that the process of modernizing the economy could be accelerated with the help of foreign countries and firms. Agricultural and industrial production, science, technology, and economic management are advancing at such a pace that no single country can generate all the relevant information itself. Any country, whether socialist or not, must rely on others for materials and knowledge that it does not possess, in exchange for its own resources. This relationship results in benefits for all parties involved.

While China now emphasizes relationships with foreign firms and countries through its open door policy, the premier governing rule is that the relationship must be based on the principle of "equality and mutual benefit." China's past history indicates that it has not been always treated on an equal basis. This past history of exploitation has made the republic very conscious that relationships have to be established on the basis of equality and mutual benefit for all.

Perceived Problems with the Open Door Policy

Some in China would argue that the current open door policy is not in their nation's best interests. They fear that the open door policy would weaken the Chinese resolve for self-reliance and lead to dependency on foreign firms and countries. As examples, they cite the situation of some developing countries that borrowed heavily overseas to acquire modern technology and, for whatever reasons, were not able to service the foreign debts. These countries then had to seek extensions or reschedulings of their debts, while the decrease in the amount of inflow of foreign debt created recessionary conditions in their domestic economies. In some quarters it is felt that China's open door policy could conceivably lead to a similar predicament for China.

While the scenario discussed above could possibly apply to China, there are a variety of reasons to explain that the probability of such being the case with China is negligible. First, it is felt that the need for self-reliance did not exist in the developing countries that became indebted. These countries made foreign aid and loans the foundation of their economic development and modernization plans. Higher levels of development could be achieved only with additional foreign aid and loans. Sufficient attention was not paid to the implications of being excessively in debt. These countries often borrowed more than they were capable of servicing, and thus their problems were not unanticipated.

Second, China has been very careful with regard to its import of technology and equipment and with its joint ventures. China has acquired its foreign technology, capital, and knowledge with its special needs and conditions in mind. Such has not been the case with many of the developing countries that went into debt. Their choice of the particular technology, capital, and knowledge was not the most appropriate in some cases.

Third, many of these developing countries based their development strategies on servicing foreign markets. They would quite often obtain the raw materials for production from abroad and then try to sell the goods manufactured overseas. The success of these strategies was affected by a wide variety of factors, including exchange rates, tastes and preferences of overseas customers, and export-import policies of foreign governments. By contrast, while China actively engages in exports, the focus of its development is not based on production for overseas markets. Technology, capital, and knowledge acquired from abroad are primarily for the benefit of Chinese. Thus, China does not have to be dependent on the caprices of others for its open door policy to succeed.

Finally, China is a country that has an abundance of natural resources. It does not have to depend on other nations for sources of raw materials.

All the factors discussed above lead to the conclusion that China can maintain an open door policy without losing its independence or self-reliance.

Open Door Policy and the Economy

Some in China have argued that the open door policy will adversely affect China's economy. In fact, this observation is based on fact. During 1977–78 China imported a large amount of equipment, including unneeded and at times duplicate equipment. Also, consumer goods appear to have been imported indiscriminately. The result was that a variety of domestic industries were adversely affected. Does this imply that China's open door policy could, in fact, adversely affect its economic development?

The answer lies in the policies pursued by China since 1978. For one, coordination in equipment purchases has almost eradicated the need to acquire unnecessary equipment. By far and large, only technologically advanced equipment is procured.

Second, rather than emphasizing purchase of complete sets of equipment, the focus now is on purchasing only those parts that cannot be manufactured domestically. Thus, imports of items that China can produce itself are restricted. Similarly, imports of consumer goods are restricted also.

Finally, China has put into effect a coordinated export-import policy. Priority is given to importing high technology and technologically complex items. Import of materials is restricted to those that China cannot produce itself or those that are highly important for its industrial and agricultural production base. Thus, China can follow an open door policy without hurting its economy.

Open Door Policy and the Third World

As China strives to develop its economy, a natural question to ask is whether ultimately China will leave the ranks of Third World countries and view itself as a developed nation. Third World countries have a tendency to describe developed nations in terms of hegemonism, imperialism, and colonialism. To date, China has viewed itself as a Third World country and has cooperated with other Third World countries through a variety of mechanisms such as economic and technological linkages.

Chinese officials have articulated four principles in China's relationships with other Third World countries. These principles are equality and mutual benefit, emphasis on practical results, adoption of various forms of mutual cooperation, and mutual development. China feels that it has much in common with Third World countries in terms of the economic system, the level of development and technology, and the need for raising the standard of living. Thus, China feels that it and the other Third World countries can learn much from each other.

China has continued to seek ways to strengthen its relationships with Third World countries. It views natural resources within itself and in other Third World countries as bases for expanding Third World trade. It is also looking for ways to expand transfer of technology within the Third World.

China has emphasized its self-reliance at the same time that it has sought to increase the well-being of the Chinese people. The republic followed the open door policy to achieve its social and economic goals. In the meantime, it has continued to emphasize and strengthen its relationships with the Third World countries. China will continue to view itself as a Third World country and will continue to promote mutual benefit and friendship.

EMPLOYMENT CREATION

As is typical with many developing economies, China has a tremendous need to create employment. It has no shortage of natural resources to establish a technological economy, but it does suffer from a shortage of capital and technological know-how. China has identified industrial development as the vehicle for creating new jobs in the economy. During the First Five-Year Plan, its capital expenditures totaled 55 billion yuan. Over two-thirds of the expenditures went toward expanding the industrial productive capacity and building up the industrial infrastructure. (The remaining expenditures were for housing, hospitals, schools, and so forth.) While this level of expenditure placed a heavy burden on China, it did provide for employment creation.

Even three decades after the First Five-Year Plan, China's emphasis on industrialization as a basis for employment creation has not changed. Joint ventures that hold the promise for creating net new employment opportunities for the Chinese are given high priority. Joint ventures that are labor-intensive are preferred to capital-intensive ventures, provided that tradeoffs for the technological benefits are reasonable.

A second factor with employment creation is that China prefers to emphasize training over welfare aid. Joint ventures that hold the promise of providing new types of training, technical or otherwise, for Chinese are given higher priority than ventures that can effectively utilize the existing level of artisanship in China. Firms considering joint ventures in China may want to give serious consideration to incorporating appropriate training programs for their potential Chinese employees.

A third employment factor is that China wants to stem the flow of workers from the rural to urban areas. The existing supply of labor in urban areas is placing great pressures on Chinese society. Joint ventures that emphasize setting up plants in nonurban or agricultural areas are not only deemed desirable, but in fact are eligible for especially favorable tax treatment. For example, joint ventures that emphasize artistic and handicraft products are highly desirable.

INFRASTRUCTURE AND ENERGY

China's infrastructure can be considered to be rather dated. China is particularly concerned with its transportation system, its harbors, its communications system, and so forth. Joint ventures that can help update the infrastructure are eagerly considered by Chinese officials. This does not mean that China is going to allow a foreign firm to provide domestic transportation or telecommunications. It does mean that China will seriously consider joint ventures that can help the republic improve its infrastructure without damaging its sovereignty.

Similarly, in the extractive and energy resources areas (coal, oil, electric power, nonferrous metals), China is willing to consider those joint ventures that can help it in developing these resources. For example, the Southwest Resources Development Company is looking to set up joint ventures. In the Guizhou Province, for example, extraction of coal and other minerals is going to require billions of dollars in investments. Oil fields in Bohai and South China also require heavy capital investments. In all of these areas, foreign capital is especially needed and welcome. It should be noted parenthetically that firms from Japan and France appear to have a head start over firms from other countries.

TRANSFER OF TECHNOLOGY

   Transfer of technology can occur in a variety of ways. One of the more frequently used methods in the United States is the use of management consultants. Firms that may not have a certain type of expertise within the firm, or that are interested in evaluation of the validity of their internal decisions, will quite often resort to the use of external consultants. Consultants can serve as conduits for the transfer of technology, quite often managerial, that may not exist within the firm. The practice of utilizing their services is well established in the United States. In China, however, management consultants are generally not used for three reasons. First, the practice of using consultants is not well known in China, and thus the Chinese shy away from using their services. Second, consultants typically charge fees that, on a daily basis, can exceed a Chinese worker's salary for a year. Therefore, Chinese officials find it hard to justify the use of consultants. A third reason is that many firms, with the expectation of establishing Chinese ties, are more than willing to provide a certain amount of consulting-type services for free. Overall, then, when consultants charge for their services, the Chinese do not make much use of them as a method for acquiring foreign technology. Not much change can be expected in the near future.
   A second method for the transfer of technology is through licensing arrangements. Chinese firms, for example, could license processes to manufacture goods in China and pay for the licenses through royalties. Unfortunately, China does not subscribe to patent and copyright arrangements. As a result, foreign firms are reluctant to sign licensing agreements with Chinese firms because they

are concerned that their proprietary rights may not be adequately protected. Actually, there is some substance to this concern, because, in the past, in some circumstances, certain Chinese firms have duplicated copyrighted or patented products.

Part of the reason that some Chinese firms have produced patented products has to do with the economic and political environment. At times China either did not have sufficient foreign exchange or did not have sufficient access to trade channels to allow it to purchase replacement and/or repair parts. In these situations, whenever possible, these parts were reproduced domestically to maintain vital operations. Another reason is that not only in China but in many other Third World countries the prevailing feeling is that items or processes should exist in the public domain and thus should not be patented or copyrighted. Examples are computers, drugs, chemicals, and fertilizers.

For the reasons discussed, it is felt that licensing will not contribute significantly to the transfer of technology to China in the near future. It may be that as China develops its own technology and examines the issues of giving it away free, or earning foreign exchange by licensing it, it may decide that the time has come for it to develop its own patent and copyright policies and perhaps even to become a signatory to worldwide agreements.

Another method for the transfer of technology is through joint ventures. In a Chinese-foreign joint venture, the foreign partner may contribute some combination of equipment, technology, managerial and manufacturing know-how, and capital. This approach to a busines venture in China may be very appealing to foreign firms because they can maintain adequate control over their intellectual properties.

China has a great deal of interest in acquiring new and modern technologies. In this respect, joint ventures become especially appealing to China. Foreign firms, however, that are interested only in providing obsolete technology may find that their Chinese hosts are less than enthusiastic in pursuing a joint venture.

MODERNIZATION

China has a stated goal of reaching an annual per capita income of $800 by the end of the twentieth century. Given that in the early 1980s the annual per capita figure was around $100 to $120, reaching the stated goal requires significant modernization on China's part, implying an annual growth rate of about 12 percent. Modernization in China is proving to be a difficult task for two reasons. First, China has a huge population, with 80 percent making a living as peasants. Second, China started out from a very low economic base.

Given the large peasant population, China has chosen to emphasize agriculture first in its modernization plans. This does not mean that industry, defense, or technology will be ignored. Rather, it means that special attention is being paid to the rural economy. Mechanization in agriculture will come slowly. At the initial stages, China is emphasizing the gradual change of the rural economy by encouraging cottage industry and light manufacturing. Joint ventures that emphasize increased agricultural yields, development of cottage industries, and employment in the nonurban areas may be viewed as highly desirable.

China's second modernization emphasis is on light and then heavy industry. Modernization in this area is affected by not only national needs but also by the supply of raw materials. Advanced technology firms will provide the nucleus for China's modernization, but small to medium-size firms that are less technologically advanced will provide the bulk of industrial output and employment. The republic is interested in joint ventures that provide China with access to high technology, but it is not going to ignore low-technology joint ventures that provide China with foreign exchange and employment for its citizens.

Another area of emphasis in China's modernization is the existing industrial base. While in the industrialized West, continual upgrading of existing facilities is the norm rather than the exception, such is not the case in China. Quite often, China's almost 400,000 enterprises suffer from inadequate equipment and facilities that have not been updated or renovated in a long time. China is interested in upgrading these enterprises and increasing the quality and quantity of their outputs. Joint ventures that are designed to provide this type of technological transformation may find eager hosts in China.

CONCLUSIONS

Many foreign firms, taking into consideration a market of 1 billion Chinese, eagerly await the signing of a joint venture agreement as a device for tapping into the world's numerically largest consumer market. Almost without fail, they ultimately come to the conclusion that a joint venture will not help them in penetrating the Chinese consumer market. This process of becoming enthusiastic about a Chinese joint venture, only to stub one's toes, is going to be repeatedly experienced by foreign firms as long as they fail to understand and develop an appreciation for the Chinese perspective on joint ventures.

A foreign firm that focuses on China's open door policy is bound to be disappointed unless it has developed an understanding of China's need for self-reliance. China views the open door policy as a mechanism for achieving its social, cultural, and economic goals. Money and profits, while relevant, are not the sole determinants of China's willingness to sign joint venture agreements.

This chapter has provided a Chinese perspective on joint ventures. The key issues for a foreign firm seeking a joint venture are: (1) does the joint venture help China with its modernization program; (2) will it help with employment creation in China; (3) will it provide China access to new technology; (4) will it provide foreign exchange for China; (5) will it alleviate, or at the minimum maintain, the rural-urban employment mix in China; (6) will it allow China to maintain its economic, political, and cultural sovereignty; (7) will it help China improve its infrastructure? Positive answers to these questions would go a long way toward developing a lasting relationship with China.

10

The Chinese Joint Venture Law

In July 1979 the National People's Congress approved the Law of the People's Republic of China on Joint Ventures Using Chinese and Foreign Investment. This joint venture law (JVL) ushered in a new era for China and for foreign firms contemplating doing business in China. The law reflected China's desire to open its doors to foreign investments for the purpose of enhancing the well-being of the Chinese by helping the republic achieve its economic goals over the next few decades. The law provided foreign firms with a unique opportunity to do business in the world's most populous country. Since 1979 some 2,300 foreign firms have experienced different levels of performance from their Chinese joint ventures. Some of the situations have arisen due to a lack of understanding in terms of what can and should be part of negotiating a joint venture in China. This chapter provides a detailed article-by-article interpretation of the JVL. The last section in the chapter provides additional information on starting a joint venture in China.

This chapter is based on a working paper by the authors and Lynette L. Knowles of Ohio State University.

JOINT VENTURE LAW

The joint venture law is written in Chinese. An informal or unofficial translation is provided by *Xinhua*, the New China News Agency. The JVL has 15 articles that are interpreted below paragraph by paragraph.

Article 1

With a view to expanding international economic cooperation and technological exchange, the People's Republic of China permits foreign companies, enterprises, other economic entities, or individuals (hereinafter referred to as foreign participants) to incorporate themselves, within the territory of the People's Republic of China, into joint ventures with Chinese companies, enterprises, or other economic entities (hereinafter referred to as Chinese participants) on the principle of equality and mutual benefit and subject to authorization by the Chinese government.

Notice that, as emphasized in the previous chapter, the law specifically mentions the principle of equality and mutual benefit. The JVL seeks to assure that both the foreign and the Chinese participants will be on an equal footing. Foreign participants are defined broadly to include essentially anyone interested in doing business in China. Similarly, Chinese participants are broadly defined, although, in practice, branch operations cannot enter into joint operations.

Article 2

The Chinese government protects, by the legislation in force, the resources invested by a foreign participant in a joint venture and the profits due him pursuant to the agreements, contracts, and articles of association, authorized by the Chinese government as well as his other lawful rights and interests.

This paragraph of Article 2 indicates that the foreign participant is protected by the laws in effect at the time the joint venture agreement is signed. Those who have read the original Chinese JVL argue that Article 2 refers to both present as well as future law. Given the vagueness of Article 2, it behooves a foreign participant to try to include appropriate protective clauses in its joint venture agreement.

Some U.S. firms seeking to enter into joint venture agreements have expressed their concerns that future laws may not be particularly favorable to their joint ventures. In these cases, it may be appropriate to negotiate terms that would allow the foreign participant to terminate a joint venture if laws are passed that are unfavorable to its vested interests. Another approach would be to include a clause that would stipulate that legislation approved subsequent to the signing of the joint venture would not apply to the joint venture.

The phrase "other lawful rights and interests" is also subject to interpretation. The problem here arises because China has little in the way of law. Thus, the focus of the joint venture should be on "interests," that is, protective clauses that have been included in the joint venture agreement. From time to time, reports surface concerning the problems that foreign participants are encountering with their joint ventures. Quite often, the problem is that not enough protective clauses have been included in the joint venture agreement.

The JVL is silent on issues that are not covered by either the JVL or the joint venture agreement. The JVL is still too new to allow one to draw any meaningful conclusions on items such as expropriation, for example. Since the Chinese have an extreme desire to negotiate and resolve differences, it is unclear how, in practice, the joint venture agreement clauses will be legally enforced.

All activities of a joint venture shall be governed by the laws, decrees, and pertinent rules and regulations of the People's Republic of China.

Paragraph 2 of Article 2 implies that the foreign participant has to be willing to conform to China's rules and regulations. Foreign exchange, for example, comes under the purview of the Bank of China and the State General Administration of Exchange Control, and presumably all their rules and regulations would apply to any joint venture. Sufficient time has not elapsed to provide a definitive reading on this issue.

Article 3

A joint venture shall apply to the Foreign Investment Commission of the People's Republic of China for authorization of the agreements and contracts concluded between the parties to the venture and the articles of association of the venture formulated by them, and the Commission shall authorize or reject these documents within three months.

Article 3 specifies that joint venture agreements and related papers should be submitted to the Foreign Investment Commission (FIC) for approval. The FIC is part of the Ministry of Foreign Economic Relations. The FIC has three months to approve or reject the agreement. Presumably, the three-month period starts when the papers are submitted to the FIC.

While Article 3 provides only for the FIC's approval or rejection of the joint venture agreement, in practice the FIC may require modifications in the agreement before it is approved. This procedure then ensures the Chinese government that the joint venture conforms to its ideological, cultural, and economic policies. Practical aspects of this article are further discussed in the last section of this chapter.

When authorized, the joint venture shall register with the General Administration for Industry and Commerce of the People's Republic of China and start operations under license.

After approval by the FIC, the joint venture must register with the General Administration for Industry and Commerce.

Article 4

A joint venture shall take the form of a limited liability company. In the registered capital of a joint venture, the proportion of the investment contributed by the foreign participant(s) shall in general not be less than twenty-five percent.

This article indicates that the joint venture has to be a limited liability company. The law does not provide for other forms of business operations such as a partnership. China to date does not have much in the way of what a U.S. business person would identify as the Uniform Commercial Code. Thus, the need for including appropriate clauses in the joint venture agreement is emphasized again.

This article specifies only the lower limit for equity participation by foreign partners. The upper limit conceivably could be as high as 99 percent. It should be noted, however, that equity participation is not to be confused with effective control of the joint venture—the Chinese partner will always retain control of the joint venture. Contrary to the strategies for joint ventures in other countries, where equity participation and control are typically synonymous, a foreign partner in China should give serious consideration to a lower level of equity participation. The reason is that less is at risk for the foreign participant if the joint venture turns out to be a losing proposition.

The profits, risks, and losses of a joint venture shall be shared by the parties to the venture in proportion to their contributions to the registered capital.

Paragraph 2 of Article 4 does not address the issue of what happens if cumulative losses exceed the foreign partner's equity contribution. In theory, since the joint venture has limited liability, the foreign partner's exposure to losses is limited to its equity contribution. In practice, of course, the foreign partner may find itself absorbing losses beyond its equity participation if it intends to enter into, or already has, other joint ventures in China.

The transfer of one party's share in the registered capital shall be effected only with the consent of the other parties to the venture.

Nothing is mentioned about the need for government approval prior to the transfer. Presumably, transfer could occur without approval by the FIC or some other government agency. In practice, since all Chinese partners are government owned, some sort of government approval is implicit. Transfer of a joint venture ownership in China may not be quite as easy as in some other countries for a variety of reasons. First, the Chinese prefer to develop long-term relationships, and it may be difficult for them to accept a brand new partner. Second, the Chinese may feel that the joint venture is specific to a particular foreign partner, thus hindering its transfer to a new foreign partner. Finally, China may take the approach that approved foreign exchange transfers out of China are specific to a foreign partner and not transferable to a new partner.

All three paragraphs in Article 4 refer to "registered capital," that is, authorized capital. While in the United States, capital can be authorized but does not have to be issued, such is, presumably, not the case in China. All registered capital has to be issued. Thus, the JVL does not address the issue of additional issuance of shares after the joint venture has already started. It may be surmised that additional capital contributions would need governmental approval.

Article 5

Each party to a joint venture may contribute cash, capital goods, industrial property rights, etc., as its investment in the venture.

The foreign partner will be expected to contribute some combination of cash, equipment, and technology. The JVL recognizes the importance of patents and other forms of intellectual properties, something that China technically does not recognize.

The technology or equipment contributed by any foreign participant as investment shall be truly advanced and appropriate to China's needs. In cases of losses caused by deception through the intentional provision of outdated equipment or technology, compensation shall be paid for the losses.

China has repeatedly indicated its desire to acquire up-to-date technology. This is clearly reflected in paragraph 2, Article 5. However, note the conflict between "truly advanced" and "appropriate." Given China's labor costs, energy resources, and need for employment creation, advanced technology simply may not be appropriate for China. A look at Article 7 would indicate that joint ventures with up-to-date technology qualify for preferential tax treatment. One could assume that if China expected only up-to-date technology then paragraph 2, Article 7, is redundant. It is reasonable to assume that a foreign partner may seek to strike a balance between advanced and appropriate technology. Being frank and open about the type of technology provided is essential. In no case should the foreign partner seek to contribute obsolete technology. Additionally, only new equipment should be contributed unless agreement is reached that used equipment will be contributed. If used equipment is contributed, its value needs to be fairly determined, and the foreign partner needs to make sure that items produced will be of good quality.

Foreign partners that deliberately contribute obsolete or non-appropriate technology are liable for the losses of the joint venture. The best safeguard against being penalized in this fashion is to come to an agreement with the Chinese partner on the technology options available and to provide a good rationale for the appropriate technology.

The investment contributed by a Chinese participant may include the right to use a site provided for the joint venture during the period of its operations. In case such a contribution does not constitute a part of the investment from the Chinese participant, the joint venture shall pay the Chinese government for its use.

The JVL has no provision for the sale of land to the joint venture. The joint venture can only use the site for the duration of the agreement. Either directly or indirectly, an appropriate value needs to be jointly established for the use of the site. If this is not done properly, the joint venture may find itself paying rent on it later on.

In addition to the use of the site, the Chinese partner may also contribute some combination of raw and/or semiprocessed materials. Here, the foreign partner needs to include in the joint venture agreement a clause related to what constitutes material of acceptable quality. In fact, given the Japanese experience in China, some would argue that the agreement also include a clause on delivery schedules.

The various contributions referred to in the present article shall be specified in the contracts concerning the joint venture or in its articles of association, and the value of each contribution (excluding that of the site) shall be ascertained by the parties to the venture through joint assessment.

This paragraph states that the value of the site cannot be jointly established. The law implies that the Chinese government is the sole determinant of the value of the use of the site. Clearly, a foreign partner is not going to accept a valuation that is reached without its input. Thus, as stated previously, the foreign partner needs to be involved in arriving at an equitable value for the use of the site.

The Chinese partner may contribute labor, factory, and perhaps some equipment. Not only the value of these contributions, but the timetable for making these contributions should be specified. If possible, a readjustment clause may be included in the agreement specifying revaluation if contributions are affected by large currency fluctuations.

Technology transferred by the foreign partner will need to be appropriately valued and capitalized. This capitalized value might constitute gains for the foreign partner and may be subject to taxes in its country of domicile. The tax implications need to be carefully considered. Some joint venture agreements call for continued infusions of new technology. Even if this is not the case, but there is some potential for additional contributions of technology, the foreign partner needs to include an appropriate clause covering the capitalization of additional technology contributed.

Article 6

A joint venture shall have a board of directors with a composition stipulated in the contracts and the articles of association after consultation between the parties to the venture, and each director shall be appointed or removed by his own side. The board of directors shall have a chairman appointed by the Chinese participant and one or two vice-chairmen appointed by the foreign participant(s).

Irrespective of the equity contribution by the foreign partner, the chairman of the joint venture will be Chinese. However, the foreign partner can appoint one or two vice-chairmen.

In handling an important problem, the board of directors shall reach decisions through consultation by the participants on the principle of equality and mutual benefit.

The paragraph represents the usual Chinese method of arriving at a decision by consensus rather than majority vote. This process involves substantial time investment in discussions and consultations, a process that quite often proves to be highly frustrating for Western managers but one to which they need to conform.

The board of directors is empowered to discuss and take action on, pursuant to the provisions of the articles of association of the joint venture, all fundamental issues concerning the venture, namely, expansion projects, production and business programs, the budget, distribution of profits, plans concerning manpower and pay scales, the termination of business, the appointment or hiring of the president, the vice-president(s), the chief engineer, the treasurer, and the auditors as well as their functions and powers and their remuneration, etc.

The board of directors has extensive powers to take action on a large number of matters related to the joint venture. Chinese managers are not used to a system of much discretion on the part of directors. Thus, Chinese directors may have trouble understanding the viewpoints of the foreign directors. In general though, China is eager to understand Western methods of management, and Chinese directors will strive hard to understand their Western counterparts.

The president and vice-president(s) (or the general manager and assistant general manager(s) in a factory) shall be chosen from the various parties to the joint venture.

In practice, the Chinese have a strong preference for a Chinese president or general manager. This may be an issue in which the foreign partner may prefer to defer to the Chinese partner.

Procedures covering the employment and discharge of the workers and staff members of a joint venture shall be stipulated according to law in the agreement or contract between the parties to the venture.

China currently does not have a labor law that would cover a joint venture. Thus, clauses related to labor procedures should be included in the agreement. Typically, it is not easy to discharge workers once they have been employed. The agreement could, for example, provide for the discharge of inefficient or frequently absent workers. A clause related to the measurement of workers' performances should be included in the agreement.

The foreign partner should consider a clause calling for testing workers' skills prior to employment. Another clause should deal with the minimum amount of time that a skillful worker would be allowed by the government to work for the joint venture. These clauses would help to reduce worker turnover and improve productivity.

One problem often mentioned is the indifference and absenteeism of workers. Some foreign partners have tried to deal with these issues by seeking to implement appropriate incentive plans. This may be a reasonable approach to motivating workers and staff personnel.

Article 7

The net profits of a joint venture shall be distributed between the parties to the venture in proportion to their respective shares in the registered capital after the payment of a joint venture income tax on its gross profit pursuant to the tax laws of the People's Republic of China and after the deductions therefrom as stipulated in the articles of association of the venture for the reserve funds, the bonus and welfare funds for the workers and staff members, and the expansion funds of the venture.

The JVL defines the net profits as Revenues − Operating Costs = Gross Profits − Income Tax = Income after Tax − Funds (Reserve + Bonus + Welfare + Expansion) = Net Profits. These net profits are distributed to the partners in proportion to their contributed capital. Since many of the deductions from revenues are subject to Chinese control, some foreign partners are afraid that they will not receive a fair return on their joint venture contributions. The Chinese have tried to alleviate these fears by repeatedly emphasizing that foreign partners should be able to earn returns that are similar to returns on similar investments elsewhere. The major safeguard though is that if China engages in profit manipulation then it will see a rapid departure of foreign partners.

A joint venture equipped with up-to-date technology by world standards may apply for a reduction or an exemption from income tax for the first two to three profit-making years.

A tax incentive is provided in this paragraph. The incentive is applicable to the first two or three years when the joint venture makes a profit, not to the first years of operation, which may not be profitable. In practice, China has demonstrated a willingness to extend the tax incentive to a period greater than three years. This is an issue that the foreign partner should negotiate.

The JVL does not specify what is meant by "up-to-date technology by world standards." Presumably, this issue should be negotiated and agreement obtained prior to signing the joint venture agreement.

A foreign participant who reinvests any part of his share of the net profit within Chinese territory may apply for the restitution of a part of the income taxes paid.

The JVL does not specify the portion of taxes that have to be reinvested to obtain tax restitution. However, as discussed in a previous chapter, if a portion of profits is reinvested for at least five years, then the refund will be 40 percent of the taxes paid on the amount reinvested.

Article 8

A joint venture shall open an account with the Bank of China or a bank approved by the Bank of China.

A joint venture shall conduct its foreign exchange transactions in accordance with the foreign exchange regulations of the People's Republic of China.

A joint venture may, in its business operations, obtain funds from foreign banks directly.

Since China has a shortage of hard currencies, the foreign partner should not assume ready access to hard currencies. The JVL does state that foreign banks can finance the joint venture.

The insurance appropriate to a joint venture shall be furnished by Chinese insurance companies.

The JVL does not specify the possible situation that a particular type of insurance may not be available from a Chinese insurance company. In this case, can the joint venture obtain the insurance elsewhere? Also, what happens if Chinese insurance rates are not competitive? These factors should be covered through appropriate clauses.

In general, the usual types of insurance policies are available from Chinese companies. The terms of Chinese insurance policies are similar to the ones familiar to Western business persons.

Article 9

The production and business programs of a joint venture shall be filed with the authorities concerned and shall be implemented through business contracts.

This paragraph in Article 9 seems to be in conflict with Article 6. The "authorities concerned" refer to the various planning bodies that Chinese firms must contend with for their operations. The JVL is not clear on whether the programs filed are subject to review and approval. A foreign partner needs clarification on this issue. In general, Western firms simply are not equipped to handle the dealings of the Chinese bureaucracy, and they should seek to avoid review by the "authorities concerned."

In its purchase of required raw and semi-processed materials, fuels, auxiliary equipment, etc., a joint venture should give first priority to Chinese sources, but may also acquire them directly from the world market with its own foreign exchange funds.

If the foreign partner chooses to buy on the world market, it will find itself expending its own foreign exchange, which is tantamount to converting funds into an inconvertible currency. Thus, to the extent possible, purchases of inputs should be made in China.

A joint venture is encouraged to market its products outside China. It may distribute its export products on foreign markets through direct channels or its associated agencies or China's foreign trade establishments. Its products may also be distributed on the Chinese market.

Marketing the joint venture products on world markets would allow China to earn hard currencies. While the JVL specifies that products may be sold in China, the foreign partner should negotiate the percent of output that can be sold in the domestic market.

Whenever necessary, a joint venture may set up affiliated agencies outside China.

This paragraph creates the potential that a foreign partner could find itself competing with its joint venture's affiliated agencies in foreign markets. Again, the foreign partner needs to negotiate on the issue of competing with the joint venture in certain non-Chinese markets.

Article 10

The net profit which a foreign participant receives as his share after executing his obligations under the pertinent laws and agreements and contracts, the funds he receives at the time when his joint venture terminates or winds up its operations, and his other funds may be remitted abroad through the Bank of China in accordance with the foreign exchange regulations and in the currency or currencies specified in the contracts concerning the joint venture.

A number of points should be noted about this article. The JVL allows for the transfer of profits and other stated funds. The phrase *other funds* implies that licensing fees, royalty payments, management fees, and so on can be remitted abroad. The JVL, however, does not guarantee the availability of foreign exchange for transfer abroad. Presumably, if the joint venture has earned enough foreign exchange, a portion of it could be made available to the foreign partner for transfer abroad. Note, however, that the JVL does not prohibit the use of nonjoint venture foreign exchange for remittance by the foreign partner. On this point, the foreign partner may find that its Chinese counterparts may insist on including a clause in the joint venture agreement calling for a certain level of export sales.

A foreign participant shall receive encouragement for depositing in the Bank of China any part of the foreign exchange which he is entitled to remit abroad.

The foreign partner is encouraged to leave earnings on deposit with the Bank of China, earning interest income at the London interbank borrowing rate.

Article 11

The wages, salaries or other legitimate income earned by a foreign worker or staff member of a joint venture, after payment of the personal income tax under the tax laws of the People's Republic of China, may be remitted abroad through the Bank of China in accordance with the foreign exchange regulations.

Foreign workers pay taxes in China based on a law passed in 1980. The tax structure for personal income has been discussed in a previous chapter. Foreign partners may try to negotiate a clause in the agreement that would place a limit on personal income taxes of their foreign employees. This clause would provide some protection against cost increases induced by higher personal income taxes.

Article 12

The contract period of a joint venture may be agreed upon between the parties to the venture according to its particular line of business and circumstances. The period may be extended upon expiration through agreement between the parties, subject to authorization by the Foreign Investment Commission of the People's Republic of China. Any application for such extension shall be made six months before the expiration of the contract.

The JVL specifies that a joint venture be for a fixed length of time. At least six months prior to the expiration date for the venture, the partners may seek an extension from the FIC. The FIC has not published the criteria utilized in deciding or approving extension requests.

Article 13

In case of heavy losses, the failure of any party to a joint venture to execute its obligations under the contracts or the articles of association of the joint venture, force majeure, etc., prior to the expiration of the contract, the contract may be terminated before the date of expiration by consultation and agreement between the parties and through the authorization by the Foreign Investment Commission of the People's Republic of China and registration with the General Administration for Industry and Commerce. In cases of losses caused by breach of contract(s) by a party to the venture, the financial responsibility shall be borne by the said party.

A joint venture may be terminated only with the consent of the Chinese partner and after approval by the FIC and registration with the General Administration for Industry and Commerce. Presumably, the joint venture would continue, even if heavy losses are incurred, if the Chinese partner does not agree to the termination.

While this article generally relates to termination, the last sentence seems to state that a partner is liable when it breaches the contract and causes losses. Presumably, unilateral termination would be a breach of contract and the partner in question would be responsible for losses.

Article 14

Disputes arising between the parties to a joint venture which the board of directors fails to settle through consultation may be settled through conciliation or arbitration by an arbitral body agreed upon by the parties.

The two arbitral bodies most acceptable to the Chinese are the Foreign Trade Arbitration Commission in China and the International Chamber of Commerce. The Chinese have recently entered into joint venture agreements that stipulate third countries such as Japan or the United States as arbitration sites. A foreign partner could conceivably negotiate the arbitration body or site. Ultimately though, the joint venture will be subject to Chinese laws. The best guarantee that the foreign partner has is China's desire to maintain its credibility internationally.

Article 15

The present law comes into force on the date of its promulgation. The power of amendment is vested in the National People's Congress.

The JVL became effective in July 1979 and very well reflects China's open door policy and its need for self-reliance. It indicates to foreign firms China's commitment to allowing them to work with Chinese firms in its economic development. As has been obvious, many major issues are not addressed in the JVL and will need to be negotiated until China develops a more comprehensive set of laws and codes governing businesses.

STARTING A JOINT VENTURE

A thorough understanding of Chinese culture, ideology, and economy is needed prior to initiating joint venture contacts. As the JVL emphasizes, contracts and agreements are based on the principle of equality and mutual benefit.

An understanding of Chinese social and economic priorities can provide indications of areas where the Chinese would welcome joint ventures. To assist potential foreign partners with evaluating joint venture opportunities in China, the government has established a number of agencies that foreign business persons can contact. The China International Trust and Investment Corporation, the Beijing Economic Development Corporation, and the Fujian Investment and Enterprise Corporation, as well as the municipal governments in the major cities, may be contacted concerning joint ventures. It may help to employ the services of a consultant who is very familiar with the market and understands the agencies to be contacted.

As explained previously, the joint venture agreement has to be submitted to the Foreign Investment Commission for approval. The FIC has three months in which to approve the agreement. After FIC approval has been obtained, the agreement must be registered with the General Administration for Industry and Commerce.

In practice, many firms find it convenient to negotiate a *letter of intent*, which is not legally binding on either party. The letter of intent spells out, in general terms, the proposed activities of the joint venture. A certain amount of technical details related to the financing of the joint venture are also included. The letter of intent is submitted to the FIC and acts as a trial balloon. If the FIC approves the letter, then more serious negotiations can take place.

Typically, if the letter of intent is approved, then a feasibility study is conducted to determine the viability of the joint venture. The foreign partner may be able to provide its own outlook and input related to the feasibility study. If the feasibility study indicates a high measure of success for the joint venture, then the partners can prepare a *general agreement*, which is submitted to the FIC. If the FIC approves the general agreement, then the partners can prepare the actual joint venture agreement, the incorporation or association papers, and other needed documents and submit them to the FIC for approval.

The Bank of China and the State General Administration of Exchange Control (SGAEC) have effective control over foreign exchange transactions. To the extent possible, the foreign partner should negotiate all transactions related to foreign exchange and include them in the joint venture agreement. Similarly, issues related to export and import licenses, building permits, excise taxes, customs taxes, stamp taxes, and other taxes need to be properly negotiated.

In late 1985 China implemented new "neibu gui-ding" or internal regulations related to structuring joint ventures. Prior to this regulation, some joint ventures were structured such that foreign firms were providing very little in equity capital. These thinly capitalized firms were particularly affected by changes in the business environment and were prone to the risks of bankruptcy. Keeping these factors in mind, the Chinese government imposed minimum equity requirements. For joint ventures with capitalization below $3 million, no debt is allowed. For joint ventures with capitalization of $3 million to $10 million, total debt capital cannot exceed 50 percent of total capitalization. For joint ventures between $10 million and $30 million, the ratio of debt to equity cannot exceed 2:1. For joint ventures over $30 million, the upper ratio limit is 3:1.

CONCLUSIONS

Until 1978 foreign investment in China was not possible. Then, with the implementation of the JVL, foreign investments were allowed in China, signaling a new phase in China's international economic relations. Some foreign firms have been able to enter into these joint venture agreements very successfully, while others have been very frustrated with the results achieved to date. Understanding the ideological, cultural, and economic perspectives in China goes a long way toward developing satisfying business relationships in China.

Between 1979 and 1984, 1,100 joint ventures were formed in China. Over 1,000 were formed in 1985 alone. U.S. firms had invested approximately $1 billion in over 100 joint ventures in China by late 1985. Joint ventures in China should continue to flourish and grow as long as they are based on equality and mutual benefit.

11

Foreign Partner's Perspectives on Joint Ventures

After China opened its doors to foreign investments in 1979, many foreign firms rushed in to start joint ventures. Nike Inc. was attracted to China's relatively low labor costs but did not fully realize the level of worker skills. One of its factories was producing shoes of such low quality that for a time only 20 percent of the factory output was meeting the quality standards established by Nike. While planning to shift additional production to China, Nike has to account for the lower output of shoes per worker per hour in China as compared to other Asian countries.

Other Western firms in China have encountered similar problems, leading Winston Lord, the U.S. ambassador to China, to state that, "many business people are frustrated by high costs, price gouging, tight foreign-exchange controls, limited access to the Chinese foreign market, bureaucratic foot-dragging, lack of qualified local personnel, and unpredictability" ("Firms Doing Business in China Are Stymied by Costs and Hassles," *Wall Street*

This chapter is based on a working paper by the authors and Lynette L. Knowles of Ohio State University.

Journal, July 17, 1986, p. 1). Some of the problems mentioned by Ambassador Lord simply point to a lack of understanding of the Chinese perspective, as discussed in a previous chapter. For example, it was never China's intent to provide foreign firms with access to its domestic market.

Some of the other problems mentioned above may be related to the eagerness of foreign firms to do business in China. Many firms, in their haste to establish themselves in the Chinese manufacturing market, forgot how to negotiate a reasonable agreement. This led observers to conclude that the Chinese take the P.T. Barnumian perspective that "there's a foreigner born every day."

As the above incidents indicate, foreign partners constituting the first wave going into China have generally tended not to fare well. Firms venturing into China now have to be more discerning to achieve their targeted rates of return. This chapter provides a look at the foreign partner's perspectives on joint ventures in China. The first section provides a historical perspective on joint ventures. The second contains an explanation of why firms are attracted to overseas joint ventures. The last section provides a detailed explanation of the factors that foreign partners consider in negotiating and starting a joint venture.

SCOPE OF JOINT VENTURES

International joint ventures have changed significantly in the past 30 years. In general, the focus of joint ventures has shifted from extracting to manufacturing. In the mid-1950s extraction accounted for 10 percent of all international joint venture activities. This figure has declined to 5 percent in recent years. On the other hand, joint ventures related to manufacturing have increased from about 58 percent to 70 percent, and service-related joint ventures have increased from 14 to 20 percent. Other types of joint ventures account for the remaining 5 percent.

U.S. firms engaged in overseas joint ventures have demonstrated an increasing acceptance of the role of minority owner. This is especially true in developing coutries, where U.S. firms are minority owners in two-thirds of their joint ventures. These firms have been more willing to be minority owners because many joint ventures are structured such that ownership is effectively separated from operating and policy-making control of the joint venture.

Earlier joint ventures were designed primarily to service host country markets as a method for reducing dependence on imported goods and conserving convertible foreign exchange. In recent years, host governments have begun to view joint ventures as means for increasing the countries' export base and earning vital foreign exchange. This newly emerging role of joint ventures has resulted in conflicts between the joint ventures and foreign parents when the joint venture products have competed directly with products by the foreign parents. China's strategy in establishing joint ventures is to provide limited access, at best, to its domestic markets.

U.S. firms typically enter into joint ventures when the partner is either a host country firm, host government, host country investor, or another foreign firm. In recent years, joint ventures with host governments have grown in importance. Projects in developing countries with national economic and/or social significance almost always require host government participation. About 10 percent of the manufacturing, and 25 percent of the extraction, joint ventures are undertaken with the host government as partner. Host country firms and investors account for about two-thirds of joint venture partners in the manufacturing sector.

Who is involved as a joint venture partner is also a function of the size of the joint venture. As one would expect, smaller joint ventures attract proportionally more host country firms and investors. Larger joint ventures involve, as partners, proportionally more host governments and other foreign firms.

In China, since enterprises are owned by the government, it is not meaningful to distinguish between a Chinese firm and the Chinese government. Private entrepreneurship at the corporate level, as understood in Western economies, is still in a stage of infancy. Finally, it is not easy for two foreign firms to form a joint venture in China. Thus, for all practical purposes, joint ventures in China are formed with a government-owned enterprise as partner.

WHY JOINT VENTURES ARE FORMED

Foreign firms contemplating a joint venture in China are faced with a variety of problems that they do not face in their domestic endeavors. With the possible exception of firms based in Japan, foreign firms face a cultural environment quite different from that in their home countries. The subtleties of a traditional culture whose roots go back thousands of years are difficult to understand for those coming from a Western culture.

The legal environment facing joint venture partners in China has a unique flavor. The Western manager, used to operating in a highly formalized, well-established, and deterministic legal environment, suddenly finds out that not only are business laws nonexistent in China, but that the rules of the ball game seem to change periodically.

The Chinese language, besides being difficult to master, has nuances that can be interpreted only when one is very familiar with it. The political environment is quite different from what one would encounter in the Western world. Communications between China and other countries can be a problem at times. The expenses of operating an office quite often can be higher in Beijing than in Chicago.

Given these additional constraints on operating in China, why would a firm want to form a joint venture there? Part of the answer lies in the fact that the foreign firm has certain advantages that can be readily transferred to China. However, these advantages could also be easily exploited through manufacturing in the home country as well as through licensing foreign firms. Thus, firm-specific advantages constitute a necessary but not sufficient condition for explaining joint ventures in China.

Examples of firm-specific advantages include managerial skills, special promotional skills, brand names, research and development expertise, large firm size resulting in enhanced access to capital markets, existence of oligopolies in the markets for the firm's products, and patents. These advantages can be and are exploited through licensing.

Joint ventures in China become attractive when the above advantages complement advantages unique to locating in China. These location-specific advantages include access to raw materials, and to comparatively cheap labor and potential access to numerically the world's largest consumer market. Additional factors that influence the decision to form joint ventures in China include tax holidays for joint venture profits, the stability of the political environment in China, and China's limits on foreign goods imported for domestic consumption.

In general, joint ventures in China become feasible when firm-specific advantages interact with location-specific advantages to hold the promise of returns in keeping with the increased level of costs and risks associated with conducting business in a foreign environment.

HOW JOINT VENTURES ARE EVALUATED

Foreign firms seeking to establish joint ventures overseas use a variety of factors in evaluating the desirability of these ventures. These factors influence both the returns to the parent firm and the risks of entering into a joint venture, as discussed in the following sections.

Measurements of Returns

Net profits, or earnings after taxes, provide an indication of the magnitude of returns accruing to the joint venture partner. Net profits are affected by taxes, overhead expenses, operating expenses, raw material costs, labor costs, licensing fees and royalties, and other miscellaneous expenses. Foreign partners, in general, can try to increase their net profits by structuring their joint ventures such that their pretax earnings are either sheltered from taxes for a number of years or are subject to reduced tax rates. Overhead expenses, which include rent or payment for land and building contributed by the Chinese partner, can be managed by negotiating reasonable rents.

Operating expenses include charges for water, electricity, and other services provided by a Chinese firm or agency. In the past, China has chosen to impose on joint ventures utility rates that are significantly higher compared to rates paid by domestic firms. Recent indications are that China is willing to apply the same rates to domestic and joint venture firms. A foreign partner can increase its profits by negotiating fair rates.

Many joint ventures in China utilize local raw materials. Costs on these should be negotiated so that they are in keeping with world prices. Wages paid by joint ventures are quite often five to six times higher than wages paid by domestic firms. Generally, the Chinese workers get to keep only a portion of their wages paid by joint ventures, with the remainder being turned over to a government agency. Again, profits can be increased through negotiating fair wage rates for workers.

Overall, the joint venture partner must maintain its interest in seeking to earn a fair level of profits. Failure to do so results in signaling weakness to the potential Chinese partner, with the net result being that expected profits do not have the potential of reaching fair levels.

Return to investment (ROI) is obtained by dividing net profits by total investment. It is used as a measure of the profitability of the joint venture. Typically, the firm identifies the minimum acceptable ROI on a project. The joint venture then has to have the potential for providing an ROI higher than the minimum ROI before the firm will agree to forming the joint venture. In some cases, called capital rationing, the firm may have limited investment funds and will have to choose from among a set of projects whose ROIs are acceptable. In this case the joint venture will have to provide an ROI sufficiently in excess of the acceptable ROI to be selected. The foreign partner should be willing to indicate its expectations of ROI to sensitize its potential partners to its needs for earning an adequate return.

Profit margin, which is another measure of return utilized by foreign partners, refers to the ratio of net profits after taxes to sales. It indicates the percentage of sales that the partner can expect to keep as profits. The expected profit margins from the joint venture will usually be compared with profit margins not only of competitors but also with the margins of other projects undertaken by the foreign partner. Profit margins provide an indication of returns associated with each currency unit of sales. Disclosure of expected profit margin requirements during negotiations may be useful in laying the groundwork for assuring reasonable returns from the joint venture.

Labor

Foreign partners are interested in knowing that adequate numbers of skilled, semiskilled, and unskilled workers are available.

One would expect that China would not have a shortage of unskilled labor. However, skilled and semiskilled workers may be in short supply. Foreign firms going into China should be willing to provide appropriate training to upgrade the skill levels of their workers. However, they should be aware that China assigns workers to joint ventures and quite often prefers to replace them every one to two years. While this may be beneficial for China in that trained workers are then available for Chinese firms, it creates a problem for joint ventures—new workers must be trained all the time. One way to handle this would be to include a clause on worker turnover in the joint venture agreement.

In addition to laborers, foreign partners are interested in the availability of clerical, supervisory, maintenance, management, and possibly sales personnel. The availability of some of these types of personnel is going to be governed by the joint venture agreement. To the extent possible, the foreign partner should generally be willing to utilize Chinese personnel in areas where local skill levels are appropriate. The issue of training key Chinese personnel at the foreign partner's non-Chinese operations should certainly be negotiated if it may have a positive impact on the operations of the joint venture.

Wages paid Chinese workers have often been unilaterally established by the Chinese. The foreign partner should negotiate fair wages and include them in the joint venture agreement. The productivity level of Chinese workers should be kept in mind when negotiating wages.

China does not have much in the way of labor laws, as is the case in Western countries. However, Chinese workers are provided a level of social benefits that is, in general, higher than their Western counterparts. A foreign firm in China would have to concern itself with a variety of factors related to work conditions and worker benefits. The hours to be worked, policies related to tardiness and absenteeism, and work breaks are of concern to the foreign partner. Foreign partners should be particularly concerned with having the latitude to replace or fire workers who are habitually tardy or absent.

Worker benefits such as health benefits, health clinics, sick leaves, vacations, pensions, housing, day care centers, and so on would generally be expected to be at least at the same level as those provided to workers in Chinese firms. The foreign partner may be willing to agree to providing a higher level of worker benefits if it serves to recruit outstanding workers and motivates them to achieve a high level of performance.

Foreign partners are used to having workers' viewpoints and grievances expressed through labor unions. A foreign firm in China should have an appropriate mechanism for monitoring on-the-job worker satisfaction and providing suitable channels of communications for listening to workers.

Materials

Local materials constitute an example of location-specific advantages that would attract a foreign investor to China. The foreign firm in China will seek assurances regarding the quality, quantity, and prices of local raw materials. Many joint venture partners come from countries with well-established quality control procedures and are used to receiving high-quality items. Their expectations regarding Chinese supply sources would be similar.

A steady supply of raw materials is assured if the supplier has sufficient warehouse capacity to smooth out the supply and demand cycles. Many Chinese businesses, due to a variety of factors, have a philosophy of producing for consumption. Either the joint venture partner or the local supplier would have to provide for sufficient warehousing capacity to assure a steady supply of materials. In this regard, the foreign partner would be interested in specifying delivery schedules in the materials purchase contracts.

Prices of raw materials are of prime concern to the joint venture partner because of their impact on the profitability of the venture. The foreign partner may insist on specifying a suitable pricing scheme for raw materials before even finalizing the joint venture.

The foreign partner would also have concerns about obtaining a steady supply of needed imported raw materials and parts. For countries with fully convertible currencies, obtaining imported raw materials is not a problem since the foreign currencies are readily available. However, this is an important issue in China since foreign exchange is a scarce resource and is allocated based on priorities established by the Chinese government. If the availability of imported parts is of critical importance to the venture, then the foreign partner may insist on an appropriate clause in the joint venture agreement regarding access to sufficient foreign exchange. The foreign partner would also want to assure itself that if materials are imported by a Chinese firm, rather than by the venture, the prices would be nearly the same as if the venture imported the materials directly.

Equipment Repairs

The joint venture partner is expected to contribute state of the art technology. High-technology equipment—whether computers, numerically controlled machines, diagnostic machines, or drill presses—is subject to breakdown and repairs and requires routine maintenance. China is not yet technologically advanced enough to have firms that would provide parts as well as repair and maintenance services. The foreign partner would be interested in assurances of a steady supply of repair parts. The joint venture itself may choose to establish an extensive maintenance and repair facility and provide appropriate training to Chinese personnel. In general, the foreign partner would want to avoid cannibalizing existing equipment for parts to repair other equipment.

Land and Building

The Chinese partner would, in general, provide the land and building for the joint venture. The foreign partner may not have much choice in where the land is situated. However, the foreign partner would be concerned about assuring sufficient power and water. In the past, China has charged joint ventures considerably more for power and water than Chinese firms. Recent indications are that the Chinese will charge domestic firms and joint ventures the same rate for utilities. The foreign partner may want to stipulate this in the joint venture agreement.

The foreign partner would be interested in a dependable supply of power. If the power requirements of the joint venture cannot be met adequately with existing sources, then the foreign partner should explore the feasibility of generating its own power by specifying it in the joint venture agreement. Adequate supplies of power-generating fuel such as oil or coal should be guaranteed before the start of the venture.

Western-type plant layouts generally specify a single story building because it is more efficient from an assembly viewpoint. The foreign partner may find that, due to space constraints, a single story building for the joint venture is not feasible. Higher operating costs associated with a multistory building would have to be accounted for in the joint venture agreement.

Transfer of Technology

The Chinese joint venture law specifies that the foreign partner utilize state of the art technology. Given that China has a large supply of workers and that wages are relatively low compared to Western standards, a natural question to arise is whether foreign partners have a serious interest in using high technology in the Chinese joint ventures.

The manufacturing experience of Western firms in Third World countries has been varied. Some have found that labor-intensive production processes do not result in satisfactory products due to the skill levels of the workers. These firms have determined that utilizing high-technology production processes results in products of a higher, more uniform quality. Still other firms have found that high-technology production processes are not profitable because they require much larger production runs.

Research indicates that Western firms that have labor-intensive production processes in their home countries can adapt their processes to the Third World environment readily. Electronics firms that have a fair amount of labor intensity have proven to be adept at manufacturing in Third World countries.

In general, Western firms in China would prefer to utilize a level of technology that would enhance the profits of the joint venture. They would take into consideration factors such as tax incentives for using high technology, the existing capital intensity of their production processes, the adaptability of their production processes, the skill levels of workers in China, Chinese regulations related to flexibility in adjusting the size of the joint venture's labor force, plant design, expected level of production, and China's desire for acquiring high technology.

Markets

In general, joint ventures in China are established to service the export markets. Joint venture products are allowed into the Chinese market only in rare cases. Obviously, with a population of 1 billion, the Chinese market has considerable appeal to foreign partners evaluating a potential joint venture. It may be the foreign partner's intention eventually to sell in the Chinese market. The foreign partner would definitely need to explore the possibilities of eventually marketing in China before entering into a joint venture agreement. If feasible, it may prefer to negotiate the inclusion of an appropriate clause in the joint venture agreement.

Since, in most cases, the joint venture output will be slated for export, the foreign partner will need to define carefully the export markets. Failure to do so may find the joint venture products competing directly with the foreign partner's products manufactured elsewhere. Quite often, the most desirable alternative is for the foreign partner to contract to purchase the output of the joint venture. By doing so, issues related to marketing efforts, personal selling, foreign exchange risks, transfer pricing, trade discounts, and so on do not result in friction between the joint venture partners.

Business Policies

The foreign partner would be interested in specifying who makes decisions such as how much to produce, when to produce, how to price, and so on. If the joint venture output is to be sold to the foreign partner, then these issues can be handled contractually. However, if the joint venture is going to be set up as an independent firm, then these issues need to be negotiated at the same time that the joint venture agreement is being negotiated.

Government Stability

International business literature is replete with studies of, and models for evaluating, host government stability. The safety of the foreign partner's capital invested in the joint venture, and the returns on this capital, is a direct function of the stability of the host government and its ability to maintain its existing business environment over a sustained period of time.

China, in one sense, may be viewed by foreign partners as providing a stable environment for joint ventures. Since 1979 the government has been consistent in its policies regarding its desire to attract foreign capital. The political environment has been stable and has not undertaken any actions to deter foreign investment in China.

On the other hand, some foreign partners may feel that there is a high level of *macro* risk, that is, risk that affects all joint ventures. In 1977 the *Beijing Review* argued that foreign capital should not be allowed to exploit China. The following year, China's leadership sought to discredit the "Gang of Four" and emphasized that Mao's philosophy envisioned a self-reliant China, not an isolated but self-sufficient China. This change in the thinking of China's leadership led to Chinese contacts with foreign firms and the passage of the joint venture law in 1979.

More recently, China's perspective on joint ventures is characterized by the statements of a Chinese economist that some exploitation by foreign firms is acceptable as long as each gets something—profits for the foreign firms and modernization for China. In fact, China clearly recognizes that without foreign partners and joint ventures it will have a much more difficult time achieving its four modernizations in agriculture, industry, defense, and science and technology.

The basic issue in assessing China's stability relates to how long Deng Xiaoping and other moderates will be able to stay in power. At the present time, it appears that moderation and pragmatism will continue to prevail in China. An encouraging fact to note is that many foreign governments have concluded or are negotiating agreements with the Chinese government that would provide protection to about 90 percent of the capital invested by the home country firms.

Government Regulations

Profits of a joint venture are greatly affected by host government regulations. In the past, foreign partners have complained that Chinese regulations have not been applied evenly and consistently. A joint venture partner pointed out in *Time* magazine that two consecutive imports of the same materials were assessed two different tariffs, with the higher one being imposed on the second import shipment. When the official complained, he was informed that, if he wanted, the higher tariff could be imposed retroactively on the first shipment.

This incident, to a considerable extent, exemplifies the type of regulatory problems that foreign partners encounter in China. The foreign partners should try to establish the appropriate parameters for regulations as they apply to the joint venture. For a Western executive, this may sound odd, but not if one keeps in mind that China has little in the way of formal rules and regulations.

Tariffs and customs duties need to be established prior to signing the joint venture agreement. While this has not been a problem in the past, the foreign partner would be interested in establishing, or at least understanding, customs clearance procedures and delays. This would allow for maintaining adequate inventories of imported materials.

The foreign partner would also be interested in establishing basic rules governing exports of joint venture products. Any licenses or permissions needed should be assured during the negotiations process. China is not a signatory to worldwide copyright and patent laws. Thus, the foreign partner would be interested in maintaining the integrity of the patented items and processes that it provides the joint venture.

Transfer Pricing and Taxes

Many foreign firms utilize transfer prices as a mechanism for adjusting their flow of funds in and out of different tax and sovereign jurisdictions. Western courts and laws have generally specified that transfer prices should reflect arm's length transactions. In many cases this simply means that prevailing market prices should be used as transfer prices. A complication arises if the goods in question are to be incorporated into another good being manufactured by the foreign partner and do not have external markets. In these cases transfer prices are subject to negotiation and should be part of the overall agreement.

As earlier chapters have indicated, China does not have a comprehensive commercial code. Real estate and property taxes, local taxes, municipal taxes, regional taxes, inventory taxes, sales taxes, and other types of taxes need to be properly accounted for.

China now has regulations in place that cover the taxation of joint venture profits as well as tax exemptions related to reinvested profits and high technology. The foreign partner would be interested in specific identification of the tax rates and exemptions as applicable to its joint venture. Along the same lines, China now has tax laws that apply to earnings of foreign nationals working in China. These laws need to be recognized by the foreign partner because of the resulting effects on net income and employee motivation.

Management Decisions

The Chinese joint venture law specifies that the president of the venture shall be Chinese. Important decisions, however, are jointly made. The foreign partner, who is more directly involved with the actual market for the joint venture products, may feel that it has better insights into the markets and competitive forces and thus may want to assert additional managerial authority. It may be difficult for both parties to precisely assign management decision roles to each party, but to the extent possible, it should be addressed.

Foreign Personnel

The compensation for foreign personnel, their merit increases, bonuses, and fringe benefits need to be carefully considered. The foreign partner would have to provide a competitive package either to recruit new personnel for the joint venture or to transfer its own personnel to China. In many cases, Western compensation and personnel policies and procedures are not consonant with Chinese procedures. It may be that the joint venture may have to opt for dual procedures, one related to Chinese managers and one for foreign managers. The foreign partner would need to resolve these issues during the negotiations phase.

Housing, especially for Westerners, is in critical short supply in China. Many foreigners working in China have had to resort to living in hotels. This may be acceptable on a temporary basis, but foreign personnel based in China for extended time periods need to be provided with adequate housing. The foreign partner would need to negotiate on this point. Food, entertainment, health and hospitalization care, transportation, and communications to the home country are other areas of concern for foreign partners with China-based foreign personnel.

Foreign Exchange and Profit Repatriation

Access to foreign exchange and profit repatriation procedures should be incorporated into the joint venture agreement. In 1986 the Beijing Jeep Corporation, a joint venture of American Motors Corporation, halted production for a while and almost ended business because foreign exchange for buying parts in the United States was unavailable. The Chinese government has issued assurances that adequate foreign exchange would be made available to joint ventures. However, the foreign partner may want some protection by building its foreign exchange requirements into the joint venture.

Foreign partners would expect that transfer payments involving foreign exchange such as profits, royalties, licensing fees, management fees, and so on would be adequately protected in the joint venture agreement. If the foreign partner does not have the ability to repatriate these transfer payments, it cannot earn its expected profits. Thus, foreign partners are especially interested in obtaining adequate safeguards against inconvertibility of these payments.

Auditing Procedures

Auditing procedures are well established in Western countries. Auditing allows the foreign partner to determine that established policies and procedures are being followed and that the joint venture's cash flows are in keeping with expectations. The foreign partner would prefer to see appropriate auditing procedures in place. The selection of a suitable auditor and auditing on a timely basis are beneficial for both joint venture partners.

The foreign partner would also be interested in utilizing an established accounting procedure. The accounting procedure should be such that management is provided with relevant information for controlling the activities of the joint venture.

CONCLUSIONS

The People's Republic has held a great fascination for Western firms attracted to its market of 1 billion consumers. The opening of China's doors to Western investments through joint ventures brought hundreds of firms to Beijing, seeking to profit from the vast market. To date, for many of these firms, profits from China have been illusory. Part of the problem has been that many foreign firms have not been able to understand fully what China is looking for in joint ventures and how to respond to China's needs. Part of the problem has been that many firms simply did not pay sufficient attention to the types of issues that they needed to negotiate and resolve in order to assure profits on their Chinese investments. After suffering through a number of years of low or negligible profits, firms have started to pay much closer attention to the need for negotiating items that are taken for granted in Western countries.

This chapter has provided an overview of the factors that Western firms would utilize in evaluating and negotiating a joint venture in China. The last section in the chapter can be viewed as representative of the factors that the firm needs to consider prior to signing a joint venture agreement.

12

Bargaining and Financing Considerations

The size of the Chinese consumer market is a tempting target for foreign firms. In the past, foreign firms have rushed into joint ventures with the idea that they would eventually be able to sell in the Chinese market. Their plans have typically not come to fruition, leaving their return on investment targets unmet. This chapter provides some bargaining insights about how to tie in strategic issues with the return requirements of the foreign firm.

The second major section of the chapter provides a look at a variety of alternatives for financing the joint venture. The alternatives range from seeking financing in China to direct and indirect financing provided by the foreign partner.

BARGAINING CONSIDERATIONS

The previous chapters have provided considerable details on factors that need to be considered in establishing a joint venture

This chapter is based on a working paper by the authors and Lynette L. Knowles of Ohio State University.

in China. This section will provide some integrative bargaining considerations.

Strategic Issues

The interaction of location- and firm-specific advantages would provide the motivation for a firm to seek a joint venture overseas. For a firm considering a joint venture in China, the primary location-specific advantage is the potential of servicing the Chinese domestic consumer market. Manufacturers of technical and industrial products may find it relatively easy to bargain over the ability to sell in China. On the other hand, manufacturers of consumer goods may find that China is more interested in protecting its domestic markets for domestic firms when the products, and the manufacturing processes, are not technically complex.

Selling in the Chinese market is important for a variety of reasons. First, the size of the market is such that it cannot be ignored. Second, even if domestic sales volume is restricted, it leads to brand name recognition, creating the potential for increased levels of sales in the future. Third, a firm that establishes itself in the Chinese market at an early stage may serve to provide a competitive edge over home country competitors who may want to come into the Chinese market later. This rationale appears to be the primary one for attracting many overseas firms to China. Unfortunately, in their haste to establish themselves first in the Chinese market, foreign firms have settled for negligible or very low levels of profitability, resulting in the recent grumblings regarding the Chinese investment climate. This particular issue of trying to balance market access with profitability is addressed later on.

Other strategic issues associated with joint ventures in China are the need to diversify the manufacturing base of the firm and to gain experience in manufacturing in centrally planned economies.

Returns and Incentives

The Chinese joint venture law specifies that profits are to be distributed according to each partner's share of contributed capital. If each partner contributes 50 percent of capital, then profits would be equally divided between the two partners.

In addition to profits, repatriation of cash flows related to royalties, licensing fees, management fees, and so on is also permitted under the joint venture law. Sometimes, firms providing technology to a joint venture find it difficult to value technology. Joint venture partners then revert to bargaining when a fair market value cannot be established for technology. The bargaining range can vary from zero to infinity. The foreign firm providing the technology could argue that its potential Chinese partner would have to spend infinite resources to develop by itself the technology in question, thus implying a very high value for technology. The Chinese firm would respond that the foreign firm has already expended its resources in developing the technology and that no additional resources need be spent for the joint venture to utilize the technology, thereby imputing a value of zero to technology. Any value agreed upon between these two extreme points is bound to be somewhat arbitrary.

One way to address this issue is to provide the joint venture with access to the technology through a licensing arrangement, which produces for the foreign firm a cash flow stream that is directly related to the sale volume.

The advantage of a licensing arrangement for the foreign firm is that it produces steady returns for it. Thus, irrespective of whether the joint venture is profitable, the foreign partner is assured a return. The disadvantages are twofold. First, since technology is licensed, it is not part of the capital contribution of the foreign partner, and thus it will receive a smaller proportion of profits. Second, the foreign partner would not share in any high level of profits associated with effective utilization of the technology. The foreign firm needs to develop alternative scenarios for deciding on whether to emphasize licensing for the technology that it will provide the joint venture.

Selling joint venture products in China is a major attraction for foreign partners. The Chinese partner would be in a position to contribute marketing know-how, channels of distribution, and personal and promotional selling efforts. The Chinese partner may be interested in negotiating two types of incentives that may pave the way for eventually selling joint venture products in China.

The first would be a marketing fee paid to the Chinese partner for its marketing efforts in selling the products in China. This marketing fee would equal, say, 5 or 7 percent of sales in China, would be part of the joint venture's operating expenses, and would be paid to the Chinese partner in addition to the profits distributed. Thus, the higher the sales level in China, the higher would be the returns to the Chinese partner.

The second incentive would be to pay the Chinese partner a management fee that is based on the ratio of the joint venture's output sold in China to its total output. This incentive would reward the Chinese partner for selling proportionally more of the joint venture's output in China. This management fee would be directly related to the mentioned ratio. A similar type of incentive could also be designed to provide additional returns to the foreign partner for increasing joint venture exports.

External Markets

Some foreign firms may be interested in joint ventures to manufacture intermediate products that have no external markets and are incorporated into finished products manufactured outside China by the foreign firm. For example, an automobile manufacturer might be interested in manufacturing transmissions in China for its cars being assembled in the United States. These transmissions would not have an external market; that is, they could not be sold to consumers or to other manufacturers. Products with no external markets create a peculiar pricing problem since their selling price, quite often, cannot be established objectively. At what negotiated price should the foreign firm buy the output of its joint venture?

Pricing at a preestablished percentage above manufacturing costs may not be desirable for a number of reasons. First, manufacturing costs per unit will vary with the level of output. Output levels where economies of scale come into play will result in the foreign firm deriving the benefits. Low levels of output would saddle the foreign firm with the disadvantages of inefficiencies. Second, the joint venture will have little incentive to operate efficiently since, in essence, it has been assured profits.

A commonly accepted procedure is to determine the arm's length selling price. For example, the foreign firm could establish that a third party can supply the products at a certain price. This price then becomes the transfer price for the joint venture output. A firm that is negotiating a joint venture involving a product without external markets may give some thought to its negotiating stance on transfer prices.

Track Records

The track records of the Chinese and foreign firms are important factors in negotiations. Inasmuch as the Chinese experience with joint ventures has been relatively new, the experiences of the foreign firm take on added significance. A foreign firm that has had experiences with joint ventures in developing countries will find that it already has a high level of awareness to certain important issues. In addition, existing joint ventures as well as other forms of foreign investments can be used as evidence by the foreign firm to indicate its own desirability as a joint venture partner.

FINANCING CONSIDERATIONS

The joint venture is going to be financed through a variety of different options. The Chinese partner will generally contribute land and building, while the foreign partner is expected to contribute equipment, technology, and capital. When the Chinese partner is primarily interested in acquiring the use of technology, the issue of licensing or contributing technology becomes a negotiating factor. From the foreign partner's viewpoint, licensing or contributing technology is negotiated on the basis of the impact on returns.

Chinese firms generally expect that equipment will be contributed by the foreign partner. A foreign partner that does not have the proper equipment to contribute to the joint venture is expected to increase its capital contribution so that the needed equipment can be purchased.

This section focuses on the capital financing needs of the joint venture over and above the contributions of land, buildings, technology, and equipment.

Factors Influencing Availability of Capital

Article 8, paragraph 3, of the Chinese Joint Venture Law states that "A joint venture may, in its business operations, obtain funds from foreign banks directly." The legal implications of this clause were discussed in Chapter 10. However, it may be worthwhile to consider the practical implications. Suppose that a joint venture has capital needs of $5 million in excess of what the Chinese partner will provide. The foreign partner could contribute $5 million as equity capital. Alternatively, some portion, or all, of this $5 million could be borrowed from a bank. The lending institution will generally evaluate the risk of lending to the joint venture before committing any funds. In general, the types of factors that were discussed in Chapter 11 influence the availability of capital.

Any supplier of capital would consider the political risk of lending in a particular country. The supplier would also take into consideration the profitability of the joint venture and its ability to service its debt. In this respect, supplies of raw materials, the labor force, and managerial personnel would also be evaluated by the supplier/lender. Finally, the availability and cost of the funds would be dependent on the collateral provided by the joint venture or on a guarantee of repayment by the foreign partner or some other insurer.

Foreign Partner Financing

The easiest method of financing is for the foreign partner to provide the capital needed to buy raw materials, pay wages and overhead expenses, and maintain the necessary level of working capital. The capital contributed by the foreign partner increases its relative share of the joint venture. Thus, the foreign partner would have a proportionally larger share of the profits or losses.

Chinese Partner Financing

An alternative method of financing is for the Chinese partner to provide a certain portion of the capital needs. For example, the Chinese partner may provide sufficient capital to meet inventory needs, while the foreign partner provides the remaining working capital needs.

The division of needed capital between the foreign and the Chinese partner would be dependent on their desired level of equity in the joint venture, their liquidity position, and their aversion to bearing risk. For example, the foreign partner may be reluctant to increase its equity in the joint venture by providing capital because it may feel that it may not be able to recover or repatriate its contributed capital if the venture is terminated or liquidated.

Equity and Debt Financing in China

For the first time since the revolution, China has allowed the organized trading of stocks, at a branch office of the Shanghai Trust and Investment Company. By September 1986 the stocks of two companies were being traded. Demand for stocks has been far in excess of supply so far. Bonds are being traded in Shenyang. In late 1986 China was planning to open stock and bond trading centers in cities such as Guangzhou, Wuhan, and Chongqing. Additionally, many companies have issued bonds and stocks, generally to their employees. Between 1984 and 1986, firms in the Guangdong Province raised about $180 million by issuing bonds and stocks.

Another source of financing a joint venture is to consider the feasibility of issuing bonds, or perhaps even stock, in China. The practical and legal aspects of this type of financing should become clearer over time. Initially, the bond and stock buyers might be employees of the venture. One of the side benefits of this type of financing might be increased efficiency in the joint venture.

Foreign Bank Financing

Foreign banks can legally lend money to joint ventures. A bank considering a loan to a joint venture would subject it to close scrutiny. The types of evaluative factors discussed earlier would come into play. The foreign partner would generally have to guarantee the payment performance of the joint venture.

Link Financing

Link financing, or back-to-back loans financing, is a mechanism for the foreign partner, or some other lending consortium, to provide funds to the joint venture indirectly. For example, a foreign partner is interested in debt financing for the joint venture and is willing to provide the funds as debt but not equity. It would deposit the amount of money involved with a cooperating bank. The bank then would lend an equivalent amount to the joint venture at a rate that is about two percentage points higher than the interest paid on the deposit by the foreign firm. The bank acts as an intermediary in funneling funds from the foreign partner to the joint venture.

Link financing permits the foreign partner to furnish needed funds to the joint venture in debt rather than equity. The foreign partner could, of course, lend money directly to the joint venture. Historically, however, countries have been less reluctant to interfere with the contractual debt cash flows to equity partners compared to similar flows to banks. Thus, link financing tends to reduce the risk level for foreign partners.

Miscellaneous Sources

A variety of other financing sources can also be considered. The Overseas Private Investment Corporation (OPIC), while not providing financing, does guarantee overseas investments. The guarantee may be sufficient to attract funds from otherwise recalcitrant suppliers of capital. Lloyd's of London also provides investment insurance. Other fund sources such as the International Bank for Reconstruction and Development, the International Finance Corporation, and the International Development Association should also be contacted as appropriate.

CONCLUSIONS

Negotiating a joint venture in China requires a firm understanding of what an expert on China has labeled the Ten Commandments: patience, perseverance, staying power, flexibility, sincerity, firmness, honesty, technical knowledge, tact, and communications skills. From firsthand experience in negotiating Chinese agreements, it can be stated unequivocally that the skills mentioned above are vital for successfully negotiating a joint venture in China.

Bibliography

JOURNAL ARTICLES

Chastain, C. E. "Management: The Key to China's Development." *Management International Review.* Vol. 22, No. 1 (1982): 5–12.

Reeder, John A. "A Small Study of a Big Market in the People's Republic of China." *Columbia Journal of World Business.* Vol. 18, No. 4 (Winter 1983): 74–80.

———. "Entrepreneurship in the People's Republic of China." *Columbia Journal of World Business.* Vol. 19, No. 3 (Fall 1984): 43–51.

Ruggles, Rudy L., Jr. "The Environment for American Business Ventures in the People's Republic of China." *Columbia Journal of World Business.* Vol. 18, No. 4 (Winter 1983): 67–73.

Wu, F. W. "The Political Risk of Foreign Direct Investment in Post-Mao China." *Management International Review.* Vol. 22, No. 1 (1982): 13–25.

———. "External Borrowing and Foreign Aid in Post-Mao China's International Economic Policy." *Columbia Journal of World Business.* Vol. 19, No. 3 (Fall 1984): 53–61.

BOOKS PUBLISHED IN CHINA IN ENGLISH

China Council for the Promotion of International Trade. *China's Foreign Trade Corporations and Organizations* (Beijing: Guoji Shudian, 1984).
 Lists the addresses and Telex and telephone numbers of Chinese firms engaged in international trade.
China Handbook Editorial Committee. *Education and Science* (Beijing: Foreign Languages Press, 1983).
 Provides a good look at China's educational efforts in the sciences and in teacher training.
China Spotlight Series. *Life in Modern China* (Beijing: New World Press, 1984).
 Discusses employment, wage systems, customs, and religion.
New World Press. *China ABC* (Beijing: New World Press, 1984).
 Wide variety of topics ranging from the origin of the country's national emblem to geography to wushu (a form of martial arts).
Qi, Wen. *China: A General Survey* (Beijing: Foreign Languages Press, 1984).
 Deals with geography, history, politics, economy, and culture.
Su, Wenming. *China After Mao* (Beijing: Beijing Review, 1984).
 Discussion of political, cultural, and economic changes that have occurred since Mao's death.

BOOKS PUBLISHED OUTSIDE CHINA

Butterfield, Fox. *China: Alive in the Bitter Sea* (New York: Bantam Books, 1982).
 Fascinating look at China immediately after the Cultural Revolution. Important insights into effects of Cultural Revolution on Chinese thinking.
Buxbaum, David C., C. E. Joseph, and P. D. Reynolds, eds. *China Trade* (New York: Praeger, 1982).
 A discussion of economic and political trends in China. Also covered are market sectors such as agriculture, oil, machine tools, and mining.
De Keijzer, Arne J. *The China Trade* (New York: Eurasia Press, 1985).
 Discussion of China's foreign trade as well as dos and don'ts for conducting business in China.
Kaplan, Fredric, J. Sobin, and A. de Keijzer. *The China Guidebook* (Boston: Houghton Mifflin, 1987).
 Very good guidebook with special section on China trade and doing business in China.

Ram, Jane, ed. *Doing Business in Today's China* (Hong Kong: South China
    Morning Post, 1980).
    Dated but still provides a good perspective on China's economic
    environment.
Terry, Edith. *The Executive Guide to China* (New York: John Wiley &
    Sons, 1984).
    Technical details of making presentations in China. Useful infor-
    mation on traveling needs and addresses.
Wik, Philip. *How to do Business With the People's Republic of China* (Engle-
    wood Cliffs, N.J.: Prentice-Hall, 1984).
    Chapters on making contacts in China and coping with Chinese
    bureaucracy.

Index

agriculture, socialist transformation of, 15-31
auditing, 175-76

banking system: Agricultural Bank of China, 126; Bank of China, 125-26; description, 122-23; future reforms, 124-25; People's Bank of China, 125; People's Construction Bank of China, 126; reforms, 123-24
bargaining, 177-81

capital: availability of, 181-82; registered, 148
capitalism: in China, 19-23; and socialism, 51-55; state, 21-22
Chiang Kai-shek, 4
competition, 79-81
Cultural Revolution, 8-9, 44, 111

demand, 68-69
Deng Xiaoping, 8-9

economic development, 25-26
economic sections, 13-15
egalitarianism, 44, 51
employment creation, 137-38
energy, 138-39
equalitarianism (see egalitarianism)
exchange, foreign, 175

fairs, export commodities, 110
financing: Chinese partner, 182-83; equity, 183; foreign partner, 182; foreign bank, 183; link, 184
fiscal policy, 63
Five-Year Plan, First, 5-6, 43, 44, 94, 122
foreign exchange (see exchange, foreign)

Foreign Investment Commission
(FIC), 146, 158-59
foreign trade (see trade, foreign)
four modernizations, 9
funds, accumulation and consumption, 34-35

Great Leap Forward, 6-7, 90, 122

Hammer, Armand, 1-2

industrialization, socialist, 82
infrastructure, 138-39
investment funds, 69

joint ventures: Chinese perspective
on, 133-42; contractual, 117-18;
equity, 117; evaluation of, 165;
labor supply, 166-68; law, 117-
18, 143-58; materials supply,
168-69; scope of, 162-63; startup
of, 158-59; taxation, 130-31;
why formed, 163-65

Knowles, Lynette L., 133, 143,
161, 177

law of value, 88
Lord, Winston, 3

Mao Zedong, 4, 6-7, 172
market mechanism, 73-75
markets, Chinese, 171
Mathur, Ike, 133, 143, 161, 177
modernization, 140-41
monetary policy, 63

open door policies, 134-37
ownership: collective, 33-35, 39-
40; type, 35; whole, 37-38

personnel, foreign, 174-75
planning: central, 50-51; market-
based, 70-73; nonmarket-based,
68-70; strengthening of, 64
pricing: adjustments, 94-99; and
competition, 77-79; evolution
of, 88-91; mechanism, 87; problems with reforms in, 90-94;
system, 62-63; transfer, 173-74

recovery, 7-8
reforms, economic: to date, 57-61;
initial, 61; need for, 51-52; necessary, 55-57
reforms, price systems, 90-94
rehabilitation, 5-6
Revolution, Cultural (see Cultural
Revolution)

Special economic zones, 114, 118
State General Administration of
Exchange Control, 159
Sun Zhongshan (Sun Yat-Sen), 4

tax system: background of, 127-
28; incentives in, 153; for individuals, 129-130; for joint ventures, 130-131; need for, 127
technology: advanced, 148-49; imports, 110-11; transfer of, 139-
40, 170
trade, foreign: basic policies of,
105-106; commodities in, 107-
108; credit, 116-17; development
of, 104-105; expansion of, 114-
15; methods of, 115-16; ministry of, 113; partners, 106-107;
reforms in, 111-14; regulations
of, 106
transfer pricing (see pricing, transfer)

value, law of (*see* law of value)
ventures, joint (*see* joint ventures)

wages: distribution system, 41-42;
   policies, 43-45

wars: Guomingdong, 4; Japanese,
   3; Opium, 3, 104

Xinhua, 144

About the Authors

IKE MATHUR is Professor of Finance and Chairman of the Department of Finance, Southern Illinois University at Carbondale. He has authored or coauthored 14 books and numerous articles that have been published in the *Columbia Journal of World Business, Journal of International Business Studies, Management International Review, International Marketing Review, Management Accounting*, and *Business Horizons*. He serves on the editorial review board of the *Columbia Journal of World Business* and the *International Trade Journal*. Dr. Mathur has lectured extensively in Western and Eastern Europe, the Mideast, and the Far East. He was Fulbright Professor of International Business in Finland during 1983–84 and has been a visiting professor in China, Egypt, and Hungary. He serves as a consultant to governmental agencies and to corporations.

CHEN JAI-SHENG is Professor of Economics, Liaoning University, People's Republic of China, and Director of the China Finance Association. He has published numerous books and articles dealing with international finance in China. Dr. Chen has lectured extensively overseas and in 1984–85 was a visiting professor at the University of Denver and Southern Illinois University at Carbondale. He is a consultant to the China Center for the International Exchange of Personnel in Banking and Finance. He is also a consultant to major Chinese financial institutions.